CROSSWORLD
CROSSWORDS

About the author

Alun Evans ('AXE') was born in Rhondda, Wales, on the last day of 1949. He graduated with a BA (Hons) degree in Geography from the University of London in 1971, and spent much of his early life in the financial services industry. Ankle operations in 1992 resulted in osteo-arthritis and nearly two years' recuperation. During that time he intensified his lifelong association with crosswords, solving *The Guardian* and *The Times* with increasing regularity, and tried his hand at setting. The poacher finally turned gamekeeper in 1996 when the *New Internationalist* published his first crossword.

Since then his uniquely themed 2-in-1 puzzle has featured in the **NI** exclusively every month, and he has gone on to be published in *The Independent*, *The Observer* and *The Financial Times*. Alun now regularly supplies around a dozen regional newspapers or magazines every month.

His speciality, however, is the themed crossword, typified in the 'international' theme of the **NI** crossword. In this blinkered capacity he regularly submits puzzles for *The Church Times*, and to prove his ecumenical flexibility, *The Tablet*. He creates cinema cryptics as 'The Riddler' in *Empire* magazine and even one on a medical laboratory theme for *MLW* magazine. His puzzles themed on various sports, gardening and beer(!) have also been published. In 2006, Alun was featured in Jonathan ('Azed') Crowther's book, *The A-Z of Crosswords*. Since his enforced retirement from a 'proper' job, he has also written books on golf and the cinema. Living in the (very green) new city of Milton Keynes, England, with his wife, Caryl, he has two daughters, Joanne and Katy.

About the New Internationalist

The New Internationalist is an independent not-for-profit publishing co-operative. Our mission is to report on issues of global justice. We publish informative current affairs and popular reference titles, complemented by world food, photography and gift books as well as calendars, diaries, maps and posters – all with a global justice world view.

A crossword exactly like those featured in this book appears monthly in *New Internationalist* magazine. Each month it takes a different subject such as Trade Justice, Nuclear Power or Iraq, exploring and explaining the issues in a concise way; the magazine is full of photos, charts and graphs as well as music, film and book reviews, country profiles, interviews and news.

To find out more about the New Internationalist, visit our website at: www.newint.org

CROSSWORLD
CROSSWORDS

**50 cryptic and quick puzzles
for the internationally inclined**

By AXE

Crossworld Crosswords
First published in the UK in 2007 by
New Internationalist™ Publications Ltd
55 Rectory Road
Oxford OX4 1BW, UK
www.newint.org
New Internationalist is a registered trade mark.

Design by New Internationalist Publications Ltd.

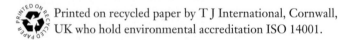 Printed on recycled paper by T J International, Cornwall, UK who hold environmental accreditation ISO 14001.

British Library Cataloguing-in-Publication Data.
A catalogue record for this book is available from the British Library.

Library of Congress Cataloguing-in-Publication Data.
A catalogue for this book is available from the Library of Congress.

ISBN: 978-1-904456-83-4

INTRODUCTION

I am particularly pleased to have been asked by New Internationalist to produce a book of these crossword puzzles. They are unique to the **NI** in their 'international' theming, which extends to the double-clued format, allowing those not familiar with the black art of the cryptic crossword setter to enjoy the puzzle in another way (see 'Concerning Cryptic Crosswords', page 9). I produced my first ever published puzzle for the magazine, which has been very supportive of my work over the years; and the subject matter, this earth and the people who inhabit it, is very close to me.

When the **NI**'s Chris Brazier approached me about this project, we both thought it would be a relatively simple matter of casting a cursory glance over the first 50 puzzles I produced for the magazine, and tarting them up a bit for publication in a neat package for devotees.

After a few days I felt a bit like Hercules, who, having slain the Nemean Lion, his first labour, was told he had another 11 to go. I recently bought a book of crosswords by the legendary Araucaria, an anthology which goes back to his earliest days when he began setting for the then *Manchester Guardian* in the late 1950s. I remember thinking that some of his early stuff was not very good, but also thinking how brave it was of such an icon to allow these early puzzles to be republished now – unedited, warts and all. I could have allowed this to happen with my early puzzles, but I am not half the man Araucaria is, and I consider now that my very first work, thrust upon **NI**–reading guinea pigs back in July 1996, was not of the highest quality. Also, having accumulated a word database over the years, my more recent puzzles are 100-per-cent themed in their solutions, whereas some of my early crosswords sported themed solutions as low as a dissatisfying 50 per cent.

It soon became apparent that there were only two ways to improve the situation: to revise all the existing puzzles, or produce a set of 50 new ones. Like a lot of people, I'm a corner-cutter at heart, and the first option seemed best to me...at least for a few days. You may think it a simple matter to substitute unthemed solutions with words more appropriate to the internationally inclined. Let me tell you that it's almost impossible to fit new words into the vacated lights. I wanted to retain certain words, so I tried to work around them. I got lucky occasionally, but more often than not I ended up having to reconstruct a whole corner of a grid, or even more, and, in the end, my pet word or words too had to be sacrificed for the greater good.

The upshot, after nearly a week of patching and pasting, was Plan B, and the result is this book of brand new puzzles, never before published. The puzzles are like those typically found in the **NI** each month. They have a heavy 'geographical' bias, but that includes human, historical, political, sociological and physical arms of that subject, thus a sprinkling of world leaders, religious references and ancient civilizations appear alongside (or down from) capital cities, rivers, mountains and seas. The earth's troubles, both natural and human-made, get a look in too.

While crossword setters in serious British newspapers often claim that 'all words are to be found in *Chambers* [Dictionary]', I cannot say the same here. Readers of this book, as of *New Internationalist* magazine, will come from many nations, so I have to ensure that British-specifics are avoided as much as possible, even though they are so commonplace in the standard cryptic puzzle familiar to UK solvers. I cross-reference *Chambers*, not only with the *Oxford English Dictionary*, but also *Collins*, on anything I think may be of singular usage in Britain, then I dig out my *Webster's International* to be even more sure. Furthermore, as the great majority of the solutions are geographical proper nouns, as important as a dictionary or thesaurus will be to you in solving these puzzles, I must advocate the use of a good, up-to-date world atlas, too. *Philip's* is the atlas of my choice, but again I do refer also to *The Times*. Further research on people and places comes from my (sadly now becoming rapidly obsolete) *Oxford Dictionary of the World*, from *The World Guide*, and more and more from the internet from such sites as Wikipedia. Placename spellings, particularly, are a headache, with one recognized source differing from another. When appropriate I have inserted 'variant spelling' at the end of a Quick Clue (Cryptic solvers should be able to find the spelling required by the puzzle by working out the clue!). I cannot guarantee, however, you won't find a third or even fourth variant in some reference book or other. In such cases, the intersecting clues will help you find the one you need.

I mentioned above that I have always supplied the *New Internationalist* with two sets of clues, one for the cryptic fan and one based on general knowledge of the international scene in the 'quick' clues. This was in part because we worried at the outset about how easy it would be for people all over the English-speaking world to cope with cryptic crossword conventions that are peculiarly British in origin. But it was also because we thought that providing two routes, cryptic and quick, into the same solution grid, would be a unique way of introducing people to the masochistic pleasures a cryptic crossword can give.

This book has given me an opportunity to spread the cryptic gospel even further beyond its parochial power base. I know that many of you will be reticent about exploring a world of seeming gobbledegook, especially when you haven't the first idea of how to unravel it. For those willing to try a cryptic puzzle for the first time – and I do urge you to do so, as once you're hooked you won't want to look at a straightforward 'definition-only' crossword again – I have prepared a short aid to many of the conventions used in cluemaking ('Concerning Cryptic Crosswords', page 9). I hope this will unlock the door to a whole new world of brainteasing, and that many years of pleasure (and torture!) will then lie ahead of you.

ALUN EVANS (Axe)
Milton Keynes, England
June 2007

CONTENTS

CONCERNING CRYPTIC CROSSWORDS

The intention of a cryptic crossword is to test the solver's ability to look at a clue, assessing every phrase, word, sometimes even every letter, and reason the correct, unambiguous solution. Indeed, it may be said that while a cryptic clue is deliberately ambiguous, a cryptic clue solution is deliberately not!

At the end of this book all the puzzle solutions are accompanied by 'Explanations', showing how I constructed the cryptic clues. The number of clue types is not so numerous, but very often a clue may be made up of several different 'types', thus adding to its complexity.

Cryptic clues are usually broken down into two or more parts: part one is simply the part which has to be worked on to get to part two, the solution. Watch out, though, as part two of a clue may come before part one, so it's perhaps best to call them the 'non-definition' and 'definition' parts.

The simplest (single-cell, if you like) may just be of two words, eg
Country bird (Sol: Turkey)
and may be called a DOUBLE DEFINITION clue, as each word can be the definition. Double Definition clues vary in size but are usually restricted by their very nature to a few words or short phrases.

The 'non-definition' part of a clue is more often than not made of several words, one or some of which, called an 'Indicator', will lead you to the clue type. Perhaps the most popular (over-used?) clue type involves the ANAGRAM, eg
Welsh town's palm tree vandalized (Sol: Lampeter / Exp: anagram of 'palm tree' / Ind: 'vandalized')
There are Anagram Indicators in great profusion. Look out for words or phrases that allude to making, breaking or oddness; or anything that suggests the letters in the word or words before or after it should be jumbled up.

THE BUILD-UP or ACCUMULATOR clue is one that adds letters and words, sometimes in a straight sequence, sometimes not (an indicator like 'previous' or 'ahead of' will perhaps give it away), together in a string to provide the solution, eg
Ultimate weight actor applied to one line in a Canadian city (Sol: Hamilton / Exp: Ham+1+l+ton / Ind: 'ultimate')

Another popular clue type is the HIDDEN WORD. The indicator is often something as simple as 'in' or 'within', but may be 'carried by', 'on board', 'passing through', etc; eg
Make an impression in a part of Camden Town (Sol: Dent / Exp: hidden word in 'CamDEN Town' / Ind: 'in a part of')

A CONTAINER & CONTENTS or SPLIT WORDS clue places one word, abbreviation, etc, inside another, eg
In Massachusetts, a sorrowful place where Jews were besieged (Sol: Masada / Exp: M(a+sad)A / Ind: 'in...place')

A BACKWORDS or REVERSED WORDS clue is relatively simple, with indicator words like 'returning' or 'upset' (where it's a Down clue), eg
Dutch cheese manufactured in recession (Sol: Edam / Exp: 'made' in reverse / Ind: 'in recession')

HOMOPHONES are clues which use sound-alike words of different spellings. Look out for indicators such as 'heard', 'it's said', etc, eg
Pass sound to get to Scottish isle (Sol: Coll / Exp: homophone of 'col' / Ind: 'sound')

These are the major clue-types that can be 'proven', ie, by identifying the definition part of the clue then working out the non-definition part by using various indicators, you should end up with the unambiguously correct solution. However, as I have said, these indicators are not always going to jump up and bite you, and with the wealth of common abbreviations and acronyms in world use (symbols, organizations, military ranks, to name a few) and devices such as fanciful synonyms ('thick-skinned type' might mean 'elephant', for instance), shortening indicators (where perhaps the first letter, 'defaced'; maybe the last letter, 'curtailed', is removed), most setters will make you work a bit harder to reach your goal.

There is one other clue type that I believe sets the top-class crossword setter apart from the rest. Some setters call it the true CRYPTIC clue, others the PUN. These are normally identified by a question mark at the end, and that tells the solver: 'Beware! You are going to have to apply a little sideways thinking here.' It may not be a clue you can break down logically as in those above. The question mark may also tell you the setter is 'stretching' towards the solution, encouraging the solver to take a little leap of faith to stay with him. The best of these clues is usually elegant and precise, and my favourite is one I came across in an Inspector

Morse novel – the work, of course, of Colin Dexter, one-time regular crossword setter for the *Oxford Mail*. His '*A kick in the pants?*' clue (Sol: Hip flask / Exp: pun on the alcohol receptacle so-named for the position it is carried on one's person, and the effect it can have / Ind: question mark), if I remember it right, delayed an increasingly frustrated Morse from completing *The Times* crossword for some time that day!*

Gurus of crossword setting differ as to which conventions are acceptable and which not. Some, like Azed of Britain's *The Observer*, promoting the 'Ximenean' school, operate very tight guidelines, where even punctuation marks in clues, if not used in the prescribed fashion, are taboo. Others, like Araucaria, setting for Britain's *The Guardian* newspaper, particularly in the past, are freer in form. I follow the 'rules' as tightly as I can, but I think I'm more in the second camp in philosophy. I find that adhering too strictly to the code of Ximenes at the expense of fluidity can sometimes make the clue boring, bordering on meaningless. My approach is first and foremost to entertain. Any deception I strive for must be fair in that the solver can deduce the answer he or she is looking for without having to take a quantum leap in reasoning or knowledge. I'm biased, but I feel that my more open style of allowing a clue to tell its story is more suited to the themed puzzle, as in this series, which, by its very nature, is limited in the scope of solutions available.

I do hope these few notes (please read the explanations for the actual solutions at the back of the book, too) will help those getting to grips with the wonderful world of cryptic crosswords to see things a little more clearly. I hope, too, that if you've never tried a cryptic puzzle before, they will encourage you to do so. I know of no-one, once the jump has been made, who has not thought it worthwhile. However, if the Quick clues are still the ones for you, I hope they provide enough of a test of your general knowledge to make these puzzles satisfying.

Alun Evans

---

* Included with the kind permission of Colin Dexter.

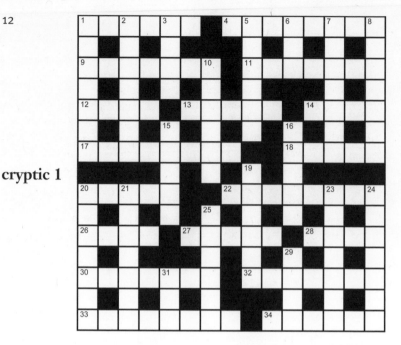

cryptic 1

Across

1 Hindu god needs to master support by the hour (6)
4 Grave solo attempt in Italy to identify examples of coastal geomorphology (8)
9 Part in Equatorial Guinea found when our Mini crashed (3,4)
11 Carrier has no right to bank in Dundee region (7)
12 Back eastern family against such a divine athlete? (4)
13 Italian city's hue after last of sun has gone (5)
14 31 of Virginia, carrying little weight, all get rejected (4)
17 Force a ship with oars to move all round 31... (8)
18 ...SOS in distress, leaving the rest playing Indian tunes (5)
20 Legal capital in Bolivia was spent in Ecuador (5)
22 To tax people nothing to gain Roman status is to set those in a new world? (8)
26 Staple of Rhode Island church (4)
27 6 of which to float yachting beginner (5)
28 Terror is audible in old Albanian trouble spot (4)
30 Ontario's dynasty, based near London? (7)
32 Ancient Middle-Eastern peoples leave as modern ones arrive (7)
33 Clue to slow movie (a feature like 3, 23 or 24?) based in Florida (3,5)
34 Cook's tour took in Australian 6? (6)

Down

1 Rants, raging about English after British discover 31 (7)
2 6 where French drink, tracking sailor (7)
3 First rate Greek character's getting mixed up with one (like 23, 24 and 33) in the Pacific (4)
5 Date after love nest's arranged, landing in Belgium (6)
6 Herb gives his name to a coastal feature (3)
7 It's in Germany where member gets one's zip badly caught (7)
8 Where 6s are found to be definitely continental? (7)
10 Most wintry here in France, right away from others (6)
15 Returned items from sales about the Swiss city (5)
16 Middle Eastern rebel army rejected a ratio of intelligence (5)
19 Exchanges blows after being in the doldrums? (6)
20 As war breaks out, a thousand land in Borneo (7)
21 One who struts has desire to return to being one of capital in UK (7)
23 Oak wain's destroyed, a Japanese one like 3, 24 and 33 (7)
24 Like 3, 23 and 33 off Iceland, the road back in certain years (7)
25 African people are at home in a working boat (6)
29 American navy ring Italian watercourse (4)
31 World's drink, in the main? (3)

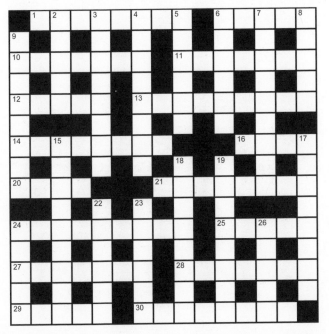

cryptic 2

Across

1 Tense call, letting girl back into Greece, up north (8)
6 South Africa-backed support is around Iraqi port (5)
10 Self-help group left tennis player somewhere in Denmark (7)
11 Studying at university in an English town (7)
12 Secret agents initially surround wood, an Alabaman flashpoint (5)
13 Man of Victoria, the solution for Canada's provincials? (9)
14 Moldova place one in Sichuan illegally (8)
16 Malaysian city's new world folk retreat (4)
20 The little woman's the last character to have a 50s 'crisis', perhaps (4)
21 Dakotas spot a pocket battleship? (8)
24 Pacific battle to capture alien and return to the Spanish American state (9)
25 Lost Mesopotamian city to a two-grand commercial (5)
27 Crazy Italian TV's acceptable in Tamil city (7)
28 Locally named Spanish resort in the French style: pretentious stuff (7)
29 Poet named after Spanish place in Carol's trip (5)
30 Chinese mob being about, row back to the island (8)

Down

2 Henry and a leading Levite? That's not kosher! (5)
3 Reportedly checks out country in central Europe? (8)
4 Little boy to visit a wide beach, one near Port Elizabeth (5,3)
5 Nigerian, Roy, goes up to university to get a degree... (6)
6 ...a degree which includes fair training for a civil war with the Ibos there (6)
7 UK parish irritatingly accommodates rabbi in a place for Pakistanis (9)
8 Scots county article by Augustus is abridged (5)
9 Comes with hose to W Sussex town (8)
15 Blood of a Norseman seen through pronounced axe smears? (9)
17 One kilometre out of Hokkaido, decoded note to get to port... (8)
18 ...one in Kyushu, where I track down mazy Kia development (8)
19 Shankar's almost hugged by instrument maker in an old Indian city (8)
22 Native American exercise, taking oxygen with fresh air (6)
23 Every departing Irish PM takes time to be a philosopher in the Chinese fashion (6)
24 Set old mass in White Russian city (5)
26 River crossing, say, in Malaysia is acceptable in northern half of desert (5)

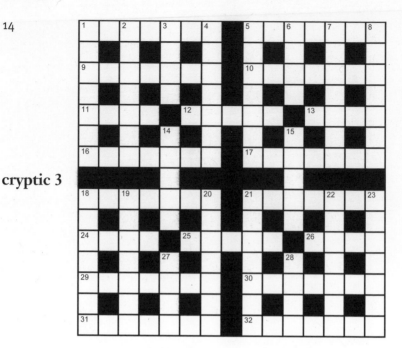

cryptic 3

Across

1 First Lady gets to sleep like a top (of the world?) (7)
5 The place in Mauritius to discover this poetic form (7)
9 Asian walks into the sun: god in Transylvanian parts! (7)
10 Swan caught in downpour on the way back to islands (7)
11 Solitaire's left out (or not?), in return to Nevadan resort (4)
12 The first person in France to get hot announcement on the Islamic war (5)
13 See 19 Down
16 Saar VAT's unreasonable in such manifestations (7)
17 Silent, anonymous banks to Northern Ireland's river (7)
18 Middle Eastern-sounding train stop by one Indian border (7)
21 View country NW of Berne: its lakes are features (7)
24 Middle Eastern royal family settling into Nassau district (4)
25 One date's uncommon, little found in an Algerian oasis (5)
26 Maybe the key needed to enter this US university? (4)
29 Atlantic island that invented republican extremists (7)
30 UK aides deployed in the Basque Country (7)
31 Caribbean island fellow's in the communist famous list (7)
32 One of Islam states separatists' old verse must be read back (7)

Down

1 Italy before the Romans is an oddly true state in the rising (7)
2 Tree in a yard is overlooking an Egyptian city (2,5)
3 Irish water bird (4)
4 Point moved first: nearly all Scottish dynasty, for instance, are Africans (7)
5 Article in the constitution of secret societies exposes Pacific people (7)
6 American (the southern half)'s curious take on civilization (4)
7 Part of the Levant embargo is, during Christmas, lifted (7)
8 Excavate ore in rent site west of Monterrey (7)
14 A thousand hide behind front of Indian building; one's from central Asia (7)
15 Biblical settlement leads to a witchhunt in Massachusetts (5)
18 Money lake is cited for disputed Asian land (7)
19/13 Slight collateral damage, perhaps, as US army fight with a certain reservation? (7,4)
20 Princess at home overlooks a large part of the Mid West (7)
21 Curry, sesame one, is Thai (7)
22 S American dry spot where a temperature may lead to a cold, to a degree (7)
23 Sounds like the Fourth Team's to meet up near Chester (7)
27 Name after feature on fish's back and nationality (4)
28 Way to explore the best Italian wine (4)

cryptic 4

Across

1 Vehicle little girl finds very loud in Welsh town (7)
5 Middleman rearing sheep in S Africa for Eritrean capital (6)
8 Exhortation to a chap in part of Arabia (4)
9 Vanuatuan island's oriental destiny (5)
10 See, say, part of an old county in Scotland (4)
11 Tear gas elk straying to find water in America (5,5)
12 Irish port bottle's stopper (4)
13 Herd Kazakh put together, lost a thousand finding uranium in Iranian mountain (6,3)
15 French city's hot stuff... (5)
17 ...its delicate silk being well utilized going back a bit? (5)
19 Place Lewis has definitely not visited on road to Oregon? (9)
21 Sanctimonious self-help group seen around Samoan capital (4)
22 He dumps Raj's rebel Bihari city (10)
24 Saharan channel maybe for the ship of the desert... (4)
25 ...Italian channel's in Pennsylvania and somewhere in Cape Verde Is (5)
26 A spirit returns to Asian waterway... (4)
27 ...a popular Chinese family sail around the island... (6)
28 ...go round it again, and dock on Honshu (7)

Down

1 Copper hits doctor over atmosphere in a part of N England (7)
2 Welsh valley, hospital gone, evacuates a large number to a place in Spain (5)
3 Rhine lost out at last, leaving Ruhr town... (8)
4 ...to affirm tank run's arranged this morning for another German location (9-2-4)
5 Australian rock band? (5)
6 Boa Marcia cast off reaching lake in S America (9)
7 Soar aimlessly over Brazilian city, landing in Argentina (7)
14 Spotted dog in Croatian coastal area (9)
16 Support over chap's informal greeting when embracing Hindu woman (8)
18 Pages found in America in a French way recognize here Swedish academe (7)
20 States support a useless disputed island in the Gulf (3,4)
22 Secretary taken during the month to Orient (5)
23 Key Polynesian war gesturing attracts Asian capital (5)

cryptic 5

Across

1 Waiting with his identity on film somewhere in Kent (13)
9 Mrs Agatha Curry's reaching a peak (10)
10 Nigerian city of a thousand with a little number following (4)
11 Bucks town when is victorious against depression (7)
12 British Rail's one line through Austria's border runs to port on the Danube (6)
14 Allies, inter alia, seen in Asia Minor (8)
17 SS Tito adapted to confront the street thug from Africa (6)
18 Back America against religious types in the East (6)
19 Californian town after a drop of rain, by the sound of it (8)
20 Venice bridge to get Arab money up front (6)
21 Spanish supporter of the second emperor beheaded (7)
25 Resurfacing in part is the province of Turkey... (4)
26 ...the pollens spread to the Dardanelles in the old days (10)
27 Statesman, sailor and soldier of the French (6,7)

Down

2 National, one chap from Rome, over time gets to the San Remo area (7,7)
3 Siamese, not that Australian, is to be accommodated (5)
4 Negative power, current in N Koreans landing... (5)
5 ...in Rio Muni port; back to start, apparently, testing atom bomb (4)
6 Mongol's city move to Barnaul... (4,5)
7 ...a foul UK plot to mine sodium in a capital Pacific site (9)
8 The Frenchman's sleeve's in the drink? (7,7)
13 African's in black trade union (5)
15 Strangely Latvia through Wednesday is little affected in tsunami (5,4)
16 Mexican rail terminal's coffee bar accepted it shortly will be in deficit (3,6)
22 Place in Holland for cheese one left before adverse publicity (5)
23 Express goes to city close to Mt Rushmore? (5)
24 Scots defile one of the musical Campbells (4)

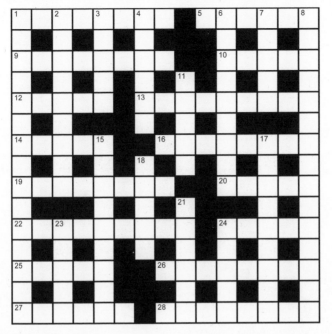

cryptic 6

Across

1 Finally put in charge of pub beer in Majorca and Ibiza islands, perhaps (8)
5 Zoroastrian's view on equality (6)
9 Organized cold water in Spanish place in Chile (8)
10 Djibouti in the old days, way off southern tracks (5)
12 Attract nearly all universities, circulating this aboriginal form? (5)
13 Lyon see EC's confused about Sri Lanka (9)
14 Range of an American desert? (5)
16 Resort to Baja California after Arab state is annexed (8)
19 Virginia's one to be found on the Thames? (8)
20 S African gold town after it eschewed lignite deposits (5)
22 Breton mail's not acceptable, first of iron, then tin (9)
24 Naive to go back to a L Geneva resort (5)
25 Got the odd characters digging up gold in a S African river (5)
26 Sheep's pen for docking in Kent (8)
27 Travel up to the north-east to a Turkish province (6)
28 Indian ascetics insist on destroying German's positive start (8)

Down

1 Erred ambulating here? (7,8)
2 Get Fritz, the director at university, to rule over French dialects (6,3)
3 Part of Tokelau's heat a fumarole gives off (5)
4 Dicky ungracious with Ron's awkward exit leading to falls in Brazil (6)
6 Turkish minority's from Asia? (9)
7 Water in America for exotic liquor; taken neat, initially (5)
8 Dissenters a real problem for folk in a part of the Pacific (6,9)
11 Dairy's not state-supported in part of Wales (5)
15 Good chap from the West Bank, one to force back the devil's hold (5)
17 Dissenting can signal Canterbury... (9)
18 ...Irish RC shrine is run down! (5)
21 Moor reported to a Turkish city (6)
23 A month in France, gets golden colour going native (5)
24 Jew loses in the end a place in Germany (5)

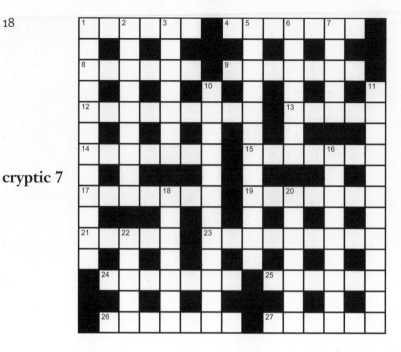

cryptic 7

Across

1 They may fly when going to a place near Reno, Nevada? (6)
4 City on Honshu where saki takes head off after one hits pub (7)
8 Alabaman town where Dorothy meets a Chinese family (6)
9 Train erratically making rounds around N American lake (7)
12 Earnest aunt finds a Berkshire town? (9)
13 Nonsense British not accommodating BT, its former subject (5)
14 Shelter hospital near Var sacked in French landing (2,5)
15 Martial arts expert traps a dog running about in Philippine port (7)
17 English at home in an island of Asian character (7)
19 Single father here in the Salinas Valley (7)
21 Is Spanish waste taken to Finnish city? (5)
23 Industrial city on the Neckar's based on noble Rhine plan, but without direction (9)
24 Manchu in fiction about British fair going to a Japanese port (7)
25 Know instinctively when temperature drops, to the second , these people? (6)
26 Moor after a dash between the two poles (7)
27 Language no barrier to this traveller? (6)

Down

1 Rule out bribes, disable compound section in Algerian Foreign Legion base (4,3,5)
2 Woolly required on the Caspian Sea? (9)
3 Ukraine city to note teatime, after the end of work (7)
5 17, maybe one, ethnically cleansed sad Belgians around hospital (12)
6 Understanding an English town near 12 (7)
7 Guizhou province city having trouble during 1000-1 (5)
10 Whips bee-like activity into a new mining town in Botswana (6-6)
11 Essex town without a car's extremely dirty and mean to a Chinese family (5,7)
16 Kind of stick date in to visit one of the Costas or old Titograd (9)
18 A company trip to a landing site in Galicia (1,6)
20 Breather student's taken, in love with Angolan town (7)
22 Peruvian city's, in the end, a religious old place (5)

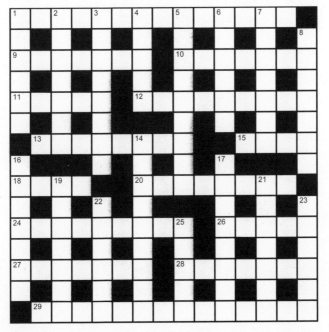

cryptic 8

Across

1/18/2 Out of London fog Haj demonstrators moved across the whole of Britain (4,5,3,2,4,1,6)
9 The wine region of N Spain? (2,5)
10 Here and in Rome, and almost all country around Italy (7)
11 A Congo sugar producer in yak camouflage (5)
12 Trail in former 14 leading to Vietnamese city? (2,3,4)
13 A star study one wrapped up getting S American capital (8)
15 Trouble one has being Muslim (4)
18 See 1
20 Beyond 'sell-by' liquors date introduced to still area around the equator (8)
24 Moving a beach and finding a Sumatran disaster site (5,4)
26 Tributary of the Syr Darya flowed back north around yard (5)
27 Algonquin Lincoln's strangely a kin to (7)
28 Old Spanish city, one striking a chord? (7)
29 Going to camp Scots composer's glen from here in Florida (4,10)

Down

1 Sichuan city affair involving university (6)
2 See 1 Across
3 Funny Asian lot, these inhabitants of former 14 (8)
4 Poetic description of lower South Wales town (5)
5 Egypt's cut the link between East and West? (4,5)
6 Like swede? Neither did Nixon: they all say... (6)
7 ...Asian meal, no entree but sweet, is a delight (7)
8 Shoot first of hostages and a father in troubled Middle Eastern city (7)
14 Crockery thrown after Party, Popular Front, recognize French colony (9)
16 Native Americans observed: small and elegant, almost uplifting (7)
17 Place in Himalayan resort someone senior in raga composition (8)
19 See a megalith found first in an Dutch industrial town (7)
21 Flying through tremor aviator reaches Czech region (7)
22 Communist capital ousts a Tory leader here in Hampshire (6)
23 French article one digested of Catholics in the East (6)
25 Pious Jew proves who he says he is (5)

cryptic 9

Across

1 Sadistically bricks up this morning, captured German leader (8)
5 German and Georgia's occupation's accepted in this country (6)
9 Uncover sham MBE involving one European lady from 1d, perhaps (8)
10 Sponsor a deal partly in a Romanian city (6)
12 Get heading off a Scottish island to the north to go to another (5)
13 Point in Turkey to Ali's desire to become socially acceptable (4,5)
14 Name a painter in Japan (6)
16 Muslim calm is all around the first person to be analyzed (7)
19 About to get into commercial backing for a Caribbean island (7)
21 Trig points for mapping, for example, part of Queensland (6)
23 The French Embassy's criticized for landing in Guadeloupe (3,6)
25 Three points one can enter a place in Italy (5)
26 Take American student before reaching West Bank city (6)
27 GI Eloise fell for in a typically Belgian way (8)
28 State of appeal throughout Alabama (6)
29 Five outstanding dandies gather round a place north of Paris (8)

Down

1 Cinema flop a year for Bollywood's headquarters of old (6)
2 Uzbek city has a line in desert material (9)
3 French chap splits to go to emirate city (2,3)
4 I'm Zico: I'm Brazilian and am at home here, where they speak Portuguese... (7)
6 ...I'm Giuseppe: I'm Italian and revolting! (9)
7 Turn up in bar, after evacuating Nigeria, in Moroccan port (5)
8 A millinery firm's only marginally unsuccessful in Mexican city (8)
11 The first iron bridge remains in Oman, on the road to 3 (4)
15 German site for UK's carbon waste (9)
17 Number in collieries get occupational therapy: a requirement of this state? (9)
18 Serendipitous discovery by the East India Co? (3,5)
20 Master the central fall first in a struggle on a Crimean river (4)
21 Actors lie low in Spain (7)
22 Sailors reach American city of St Paul (6)
24 Native Israeli gets S African support (5)
25 First of students to reach, for example, Oxford University's site in Mali (5)

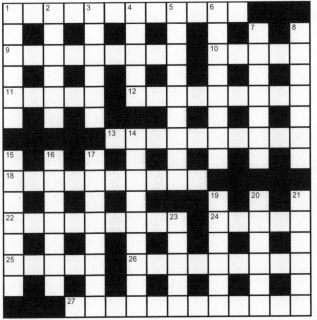

cryptic 10

Across

1 Dale Buchanan's plan for old Botswana (12)
9 Exchanging old German duchy for new in Canada? (9)
10 Sporty vehicle runs over a bird in a Belgian town... (5)
11 ...roundabout, to speed to airport for Chicago (5)
12 Polar cart used in caper (9)
13 Criticize British deporting of rabbis during the morning for thoughts on unification in the Middle East (3-7)
18 Lose American somewhere between port in Chile and one in Costa Rica (10)
22 Soviet name Kazakh city after northern sea goose, they say (9)
24 Vanuatu's island maybe saturated in drugs (5)
25 He left heathen anarchy for St Illtud's place in South Wales... (5)
26 ...or New South Wales, perhaps, finding it similar in Tyneside? (9)
27 Rock's characteristic of waters around Baffin I (6,6)

Down

1 City of the Phoenicians Romans renamed after slobby sorts (6)
2 Mongol warrior prince mentioned in French Upanishad passage (6)
3 Cloaking the Irish troubles here? (6)
4 6 half-abandoned, half-converted a currency in the country (5)
5 Atlas Kane used to find the source of the Blue Nile, as it was called (4,5)
6 W African river where Scot went under... (8)
7 ...describing distributaries: 6's river has one hundred downstream from island (7)
8/21 A more tranquil-sounding place: after a time due at S American hot spot (7,6)
14 American writes a number in the mountains (9)
15 A new beginning's declared around a part of Washington (7)
16 Whose fault is it in California when a good chap leaves? (7)
17 Execute a dynasty here in China (8)
19 Wine, the French say, needs time in the Beirut area (6)
20 Virginia's not going to join self-help group's place north of Helsinki (6)
21 See 8
23 Note aquatic bird seen at the Nile site (5)

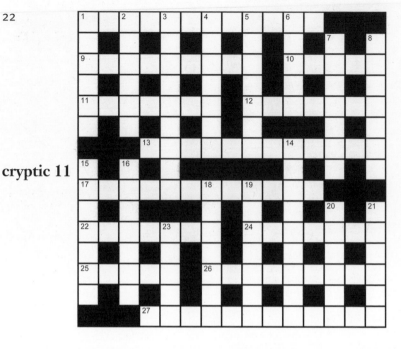

cryptic 11

Across

1 Tactical IKEA move to S American waterfront? (4,8)
9 This European no longer takes a cheque, it's reported? (9)
10 Somewhere in Henan province acceptable hole is made (5)
11 Spaniards' queen is ousted and leading Zenists come in from the Balearics (7)
12 Money lake cited for land in dispute (7)
13 Vineries and rye cultivated alongside one Asian waterway (5,7)
17 A blockade, a gun being shot initially at a cove on the Rio coastline (9,3)
22 It's a Danish island the French Academy state (7)
24 US peak gets heavier downpour (7)
25 Part of Turkey where a Martial arts expert gets accepted (5)
26 Transport a superior chap nearly to a historic Spanish city (9)
27 Peer advances unconvincingly to the Atlantic islanders (4,8)

Down

1 Whip ten in Burmese city... (6)
2 ...declaring queue to work with ten in part of Finland (6)
3 Place in Madagascar to grow almost into African (9)
4 Attempts to time evacuation from Italian city (7)
5 A nose around railway capital of W Africa (7)
6 Some Britons initially conquered eastern lands, then Scotland (5)
7 Pro-Mao agitator's head of state in Taiwan? (7)
8 The state of the Caucasus is on my mind? (7)
14 Where in Africa a small measure by a misguided chap from 25's no good as an opener (9)
15 A seabird nearly gains the current off Mozambique (7)
16 As war breaks out, a thousand land in Borneo (7)
18 Gorgeous river and department in France? (7)
19 Hair-drier's contents are somewhere in Scotland (7)
20 Horse I note in a Burundi city (6)
21 Breeding ground in Norfolk for gangsters' molls? (6)
23 A French valley Aquitaine first turned over, now part of Euskadi (5)

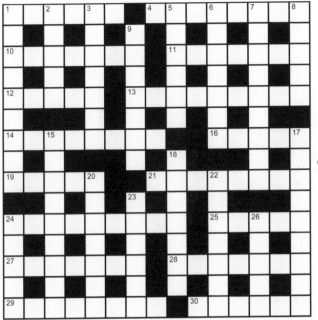

cryptic 12

Across

1 See 27
4 Touring via 28 to take in the poles, without a stop on the Nile (5,3)
10 Desert-like island off Ireland has westerly returning (7)
11 Siberian naval base views Massachusetts to Georgia with buoy (7)
12 Odd metal Americans explore somewhere in Shandong province (5)
13 Language of the first man to get to a summit in Sri Lanka (5,4)
14 He sounds on the straight and narrow in Chile? (8)
16 Fathom out continent's Pacific port (5)
19 It flows in German, Wagner's work, but lacks something precious (5)
21 National Theatre introduced Lear by playing here in Malawi (8)
24 Bushmen keen to hit Old Testament tabernacle first (9)
25 Canadian wins a night in Paris (5)
27&1 Old colonial islands where librettist is met with a measure of coolness (7&6)
28 Chap from 13, a Western Australian visiting 18 in Africa (7)
29 Little girl's sharp in cotton trousers from China (8)
30 French landing on the west coast with sial moving (6)

Down

1 Estimator of Indonesia's loss? (4,5)
2 Mullah tight-lipped travelling through Finnish town (5)
3 WWI battle in Chile's over in the heart-land at first (7)
5 S African gripe attributed to South Sea island (6)
6 A dignified first place at the home of Georgian golf (7)
7 Avoid this urban area in Kansas? (5,4)
8 Onset of snow demands a fur wrap here in Belarus (5)
9 With new bearings, leaving troubled 4 for the islands (7)
15 More, alternatively, take the route of the Caledonian canal? (5,4)
17 Winds insulate a Pacific island chain (9)
18 Jos gets state capital for this part of Nigeria's highland (7)
20 Zulu's been led astray (7)
22 Go round it again, and dock on Honshu (7)
23 American island nation makes a point (6)
24 Place in Germany where heroin middleman gets information (5)
26 A conflict acceptable, in retrospect, to a Japanese city (5)

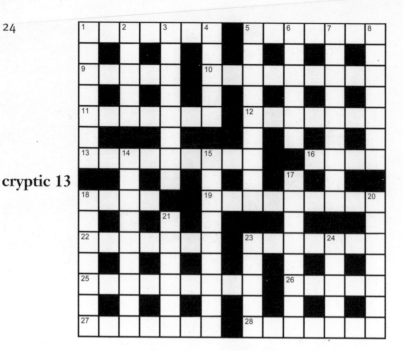

cryptic 13

Across

1 Europe backwater maybe the Garden of Eden to the Basque (7)
5 Giant iguanas found in part of the Caribbean (7)
9 Service one provided in an Urals city (5)
10 Had a Derby flutter and made a princely pile in India? (9)
11 Loftiness this may give over an English cheese... (7)
12 ...the Edam market, translated 'maarkt', no time after the Spanish withdrawal (7)
13 Old Norse antelope's here in French captivity near the port of Calais (9)
16 Back before the zenith of European vulcanicity? (4)
18 Australian's straight/sound... (4)
19 ...Turk's straight/sound? (9)
22 Pink loo blown up somewhere near St Petersburg (7)
23 Journey to find oil moved to here in Libya (7)
25 One without a majority on the continent and much of Turkey today (4,5)
26 Arab river offensive's half repelled after silence (5)
27 First Armenian Church in the outskirts of Smolensk, a Russian city (7)
28 Ancient peoples leaving as modern ones arrive? (7)

Down

1 Peruvian volcano's cloud one used to pray around (2,5)
2 Bantu points at first to Zulu independence (5)
3 Dog a resident of Strasbourg (8)
4 Tyrolean lake area, coming from a German city (5)
5 See 23
6 Hit ark when excavated in Grecian Thrace (6)
7 Kind of Mediterranean rock sound Monkees play here? (9)
8 Spanish, and alternatively, part of France? (7)
14 Sir Walter's gunners are lost, bearing down on a Hampshire town (9)
15 Croatia resort to curtailing Kurd bovine disease (9)
17 Kerala city, one near river, in, and on, French base (8)
18 Sick Arab British hospital admitted in Asian trade centre (7)
20 Good people who take English in a Charentais town (7)
21 Final word to team before going into Amoy today (6)
23/5 Caribbean islands: 'Mediterranean' types with no cicadas, perhaps (5,3,6)
24 A thespian gains nothing in elevating this Mid-West city (5)

cryptic 14

Across

1 Almost purgatory, under the weather here on the Nile (6)
4 Struggle with a new southern girl in a city on the Deccan (8)
10 One's after warp travel here in Australia (7)
11 Taiwanese city gets nothing back on Chinese money (7)
12 Directions to bypass a Roman road in a L Geneva resort (5)
13 Old African statesman's expert at winning hearts in Sumatran disaster city (5,4)
14 Girl accommodates N Europeans and an African (8)
16 Old sailor's socially acceptable in Hokkaido coal port (5)
18 Gridlock at secondary road, one leading to Sumatran city (5)
20 Asian country's type of staple: about one thousand and one to name (8)
24 Transfer Bermuda horse separately to a port on the Elbe (9)
25 Alpine peak, for example, includes ice-capping round about (5)
27 Island's anger prior to capture (7)
28 A Shinto movement's site in Nigeria (7)
29 Scots terrier breed crossed with English in article... (8)
30 ...infuriates a city on the Loire (6)

Down

1 Book of the Old Testament for Palestinians originally? (7)
2 Magellan aimed to shelter in Hawaiian island (5)
3 Six government posts in an unnamed French city (7)
5 Chinese home of Yin; also, almost its complement? (6)
6 Native Americans make a hit on a house (7)
7 Ghana's CD to Lagos is puzzling (4,5)
8 Gansu provincial capital the French first needed to cross yak at university (7)
9 Mafia kidnap male, a South African, in Kenyan resort (7)
15 Philippines port where Te Deum is played around Aug, usually (9)
17 Deposit a grand against fine, raised through Asian capital (7)
18 Caribbean island's a preserve of a CIA rebel... (7)
19 ...Atlantic island's diamond country (7)
21 Russian doffs cap to a Spaniard (7)
22 Standard, short answer? They were originally Vikings (7)
23 Scottish city's dingy, overlooking river in 29 (6)
26 Record drop when climbing up a Canadian peninsula (5)

cryptic 15

Across

1 Beethoven's retreat, where No 5's knocked out and first part of 4, near Mannheim (12)
9 UN triples force in Mpumalanga's capital... (9)
10 ...African country's sympathetic, without the necessary gravity (5)
11 View of cataract in a polar landscape, perhaps (10)
12 Girl gets water in Siberia (4)
14 See 25 Down
16 A study by a Native American (5)
19 Persian, very much, is receding (5)
20 Couple of sailors in 14 west of Sakhalin (6)
23 The country in question Gershwin's promoted (4)
24 Fly hatless to a couple of degrees south of Asmara (5,5)
27 17 cut off, forced to leave Chilean port (5)
28 Exotic pearl divers, without PR, divided chic French ski resort (3,6)
29 Part of the Western Cordillera in Andalucia? (6,6)

Down

1 Canal in Haining, cutting through the Zhejiang city (6)
2 Superior lake position Protestant half of the French supported (6)
3 Ritzier map may show this city in NE Brazil (10)
4 Hesitate, er, when leaving supporter, er, abandoned in German city (9)
5 Dick's trailing Arizona's native Americans (5)
6 German river's carrying little weight in drugs... (4)
7 ....Russian river's moving ephedrine, heroin and Ecstasy out (7)
8 Algerian oasis, God willing, has abandoned hard line (2,5)
13 Arabic game played here in Brazil's Pernambuco state (10)
15 Test old city, burying it to a degree in a Costa Rican volcano (9)
17 Continental queen of the movies? (7)
18 River in Nova Scotia originally named for a part of ancient Greece (7)
21 The Spanish table acts for a posh part of San Diego? (2,4)
22 Exploring town in Illinois as Nebraska evacuates after storm (6)
25/14 Where Britain and France narrowly fail to meet? (5,6)
26 First man after Livingstone into an African country (4)

cryptic 16

Across

1 Courtesy title among thousands given to American in French part of Thailand (4,4)
6 One is found on the Steppes, small thanks to sailor (5)
10 Back flag approaching controversial era in an African country (7)
11 Battle in Greece for Italian sausages (7)
12 See 3 Down
13 Almost time where a case is presented for an Anglo-French conflict (9)
14 Doctor belonging to us is about to meet chap somewhere up the Nile (8)
16 In Rome and Naples, one third like Vesuvius? (4)
20 Date one vessel found in Norfolk town (4)
21 Poor European politician is first returned for a place in Wales (8)
24 Madagascar resort to sorting out abstainer (9)
25 Artillery take a heavy stick to African capital (5)
27 Islands, part of Kiribati, Sullivan goes after? (7)
28 Californian city's Mediterranean style gets accepted (7)
29 Part of Siberia in the real taiga hinterland (5)
30 Fish in France, and English tea, having afternoon out on the river (8)

Down

2 Caribbean nation-state despise the English of old? (5)
3/12 Ulster's national direction comes first (8,5)
4 A Green, also known as Nationalist, being an indigenous West Indian (8)
5 Bath he built one kilometre below the holy city of Rama (6)
6 Mexico: state the capital? (6)
7 Find a knot in the Sahara: comb it out? (9)
8 Turkish leader's imprudent moving on a city in N Iran (5)
9 Stir porridge when in the Dordogne (8)
15 Rush starting to play lute in the Iranian desert (5-1,3)
17 Pacific Islands a military officer found without one Scot (8)
18 Caribbean rum's a precious sea pick-up (8)
19 From the depths of a Welsh valley to the heights in Kenya? (8)
22 City, the first in Honshu industrially, meaning every Japanese island (6)
23 Sea formed a long time ago around tidal flows, but no date (6)
24 Odd, this Khanate's old-fashioned look into a S African bay (5)
26 Front's lost: a retreat for the French navy (5)

cryptic 17

Across

9 Divide, so to speak, the territory in Ohio city (9)
10 Where in France a Rolls-Royce gets a first service (5)
11 Southern country's premier's withdrawn backing (7)
12 Tree in a yard in front of an Egyptian city (2,5)
13 Address for discerning Native American? (5)
14 Place somewhere in Kent girl's accent (9)
16 Dissenters a real problem for folk in a part of the Pacific (6,9)
20 River is an integral part to these W African nationals (9)
23 Last Chinese family in Essex town with no car (5)
24 Exotic clothing Joey wrapped around in an Argentinian port (7)
25 He led Rome in upheaval through heart (7)
26 How to report radium in a place near Kolkata (5)
27 Continental feel to a Cinerama production (9)

Down

1 S American area code UN investigated (10)
2 Asians, each belonging to a Welsh girl (8)
3 Canadian river's point where ravine constricts (6)
4 Globetrotter gets a part in 'New York, New York'? (6)
5 Advantage being on the high ground for the English Civil War battle (8)
6 Italian's mean and falsifies names... (8)
7 ...to hire within this part of Italy (6)
8 The high points of Thessaly and Tasmania? (4)
15 Old Berliner puts Garmisch first in a holiday run (4,6)
17 Retain Ur, perhaps, in this ancient pre-Roman culture (8)
18 Greek character's an ill-wind to one city near Rio (8)
19 One from the Horn, performing rite over African extremists (8)
21 French fuel scam (6)
22 Name has its root prior to becoming a modern nation (6)
23 Egyptian Christian's nervous reaction submitting to policeman (6)
24 River Rhine headwaters, upper reaches, initially directed the other way (4)

cryptic 18

Across

1 Crashes into barrier landing in Kent (8)
6 Four, initially Armenian, get on board in Turkish city (5)
10 Gun's imported through lines docking in Belgium (7)
11 Arabian nomad's head pops into British pub quite often? (7)
12 Greenland fjord where a Kursk accident, in the end, is avoided (5)
13 City in California where girl's after the right guy for Christmas (5,4)
14 Tropic Italian island's hard growth (9)
17 Hebridean place for one into breakfast food (4)
20 Ulster lough's water runs through lower Newry... (4)
21 ...British pound's out to stop the sales patter here on Lough Leane (9)
23 Scottish peak where boy sits overlooking the loch (3,6)
25 Americans resort to ski in, like the writer (5)
27 Undisciplined walkabout: Warner Bros pull out of Fiji location (7)
28 Tibet city permit S African to get lost on the way to Everest? (3,4)
29 My Spanish friend's life is out there in Florida (5)
30 Here in Texas, as in Rome, I love a little stream trickling through (8)

Down

2 Rias on the Galician coast, among basalt assemblages (5)
3 What Indians read somehow strains keen beginner joining in (8)
4 Include Russia among those in favour of taking music to this desert island (5,4)
5 Monstrous waters capsized German boat in the centre of the Ruhr (5)
6 Arab, as coming from an ancient people (6)
7 Sober Australian? (9)
8 Girl with no name recruited into Salvation Army's place in the Yemen (5)
9 Native American and joint-French department (8)
15 Write in Australia contrary line in Malay, for instance (9)
16 Greek character carrying a flower in the Alexandria area (4,5)
18 Chap seen about following a West Indian (8)
19 Hindu god embraced: surprise expressed by rector in dry Botswana (8)
22 Government's place in Comoros Islands is to establish rule in a satellite island (6)
23 Brazilian city's in the control of Mob elements (5)
24 City in Japan is otherwise less than huge (5)
26 Friend puts a rand into a S African wine town (5)

cryptic 19

Across

1 Manual used to circle a volcano in Hawaii (5,3)
6 Stake reportedly made from Aberdeen-associated stock? (5)
10 Right in time to miss gas tank explosion north of Irkutsk (7)
11 Brussels has a commercial interest in snow transport for the Basque Country (7)
12 One's brought before the French department (5)
13 Overgarment explorer's put on to make a point in Antarctica (4,5)
14 Strummer's heavy involvement managed to reform group in Europe? (8)
16 Indian city where Greeks met, but failed to get round (4)
20 Firm way of doing things by an Italian town (4)
21 Hot grassland west of river in Georgia (8)
24 Livid with million-pound hit on trade centre in Sumatra (9)
25 White wine district of Georgia? (5)
27 From Greece and a part of Turkey return to a place in Andalucia (7)
28 Russian Federation member's anthem comes after nothing of real value (7)
29 River tour around the Cornish county town (5)
30 Desert a caravan exporting heroin out of Sabah port (8)

Down

2 The early English in perspective... (5)
3 ...they harried 2 in England after Nero's men failed? (8)
4 Thousand on drugs in the French Church today seek haven in the Sahara (4,4)
5 Drink very quietly round this Syrian city (6)
6 Like the matching elements in an Italian city (6)
7 Part of Wales to see some 70s rock on the keyboard (9)
8 Turkish province developed from first southern Italian invaders raiding Troy (5)
9 Limousine? No, this car's originally named from a town in Aquitaine (8)
15 Landau Tim tripped in, in S India (5,4)
17 Attic of a Greek citizen (8)
18 Sounds like torture, heavyweight hitting Devon town (8)
19 Aid Malta transferred to another part of the Med (8)
22 When in Rome, I love to take in a club; in Ecuador, an Andean city (6)
23 Woman, Australian, is detained in Amazon port (6)
24 Sound water in the Seattle area (5)
26 Dear to Italians, one worked in Halicarnassus area of Asia Minor (5)

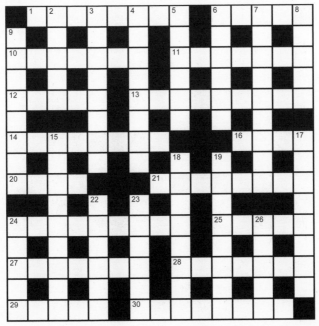

cryptic 20

Across

1 See no senior office in returning to Government seat in Alberta (8)
6 Kind of rice Irishman finds not applicable (5)
10 Article on Napoleonic detention centre's found in Albanian city (7)
11 Bomb is detailed for a US invasion here (7)
12 Italian city's banquet university promoted (5)
13/15 Arranged by Cassandra, church idyll is a trap for sailors in the Med (6,3,9)
14 Innocent? A right bounder this Scotsman (8)
16 Wickedness returns, with heroin, to a place in Serbia (4)
20 Characters leave Tunisia, maybe for the old country... (4)
21 ...Barcelona folk, men having the same name, tracking a pet from 20? (8)
24 Hard-sounding alcoholic drink? Look for water in Holland (6,3)
25 Kenyan and S African held during a month in France (5)
27 Wisconsin's legislature's raging issue is chasing independence (7)
28 One of the three 'r's in Berkshire? It must help one's spelling! (7)
29 A calculation to take king in an ancient Tigré city (5)
30 Check Slav, dubiously about to leave Ukrainian industrial centre (8)

Down

2 Name a first-class emirate (5)
3 Ferry's calling here in Flanders? (8)
4 African barrel is one with a number on (8)
5 Head into a negative atmosphere initially with Honshu's position (6)
6 Native American culture translates to Spanish town (6)
7 Anima Tao's rejected manifests in a Madagascan port (9)
8 A country belonging to Finland? (5)
9 Virginia's after boyfriend's place in France (8)
15 See 13 Across
17 Picks up wound during the Battle of Britain? (8)
18 Analyze a calibre of person from Ibiza (8)
19 Hand English boy's upbringing to Californian municipality (8)
22 Backing of new money for Norfolk waterway (6)
23 A crazy-sounding American in S Africa (6)
24 Ring to get a medic through Zambia's borders to a place in Malawi (5)
26 Role sounds more cantonal than Cantonese in structure? (5)

32

cryptic 21

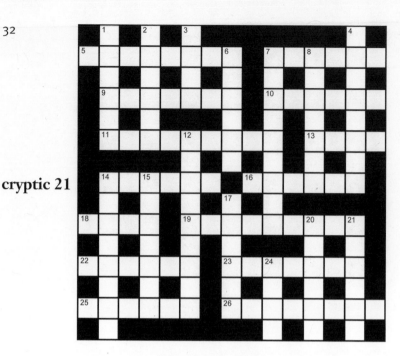

Across

5 Sank 13, being corrupted around Little Rock (8)
7 Breton river to the east, the primary frontier with Normandy, for instance? (6)
9 Almost drunk in a Moldovan town... (7)
10 ...knocking back beer to tack halfway to Turkish city (6)
11 Dog with ears pricked in Mexican border town? (9)
13 Leader of old Russian state's in speech by the Franco-German frontier (4)
14 Unimportant-seeming part can transform French spirit (6)
16 Australian inventor with zero turnover gets Commonwealth capital (6)
18 Place in Arizona like Table Mountain? (4)
19 Odd acorn, able to mutate in one of Spain's most densely populated places (9)
22 North of the Saudi border get line to stop. Sounds like an order (6)
23 British, with the French backing, secure provincial capital (7)
25 Number put to the sword, decapitated, in Aotearoa port (6)
26 Adore being in southern French department, back in the country (8)

Down

1 Detailed check and sweep on polar region (6)
2 Ubangi settlement? (6)
3 Italian town's connection with Amritsar is going back some (4)
4 One little bird sounding like a wagtail migrated to a Japanese city (8)
6 Trading centre on the Yangtze is turned over, harbouring drugs (6)
7 Virtually clear cape near an Australian port (9)
8 LA area's used water from Asia... (4,3)
12 ...Asian capital provided, from natural Ob complex (4,5)
14 Cure stomach, the innards, after catching cold here on the Yucatan (8)
15 S American folk's promise of golf, part abandoned for the second time (7)
17 Peak in the Antarctic literally before coach arrives (6)
20 Disputed area of Ethiopia earlier set up study (6)
21 23's capital here in Ulster for a n ew dock (6)
24 French centre nearly online? (4)

cryptic 22

Across

1 Part of Europe, on the continent, where Conservatives hoard gold (8)
6 Firms' safety-first approach to islands in the Indian Ocean (5)
10 Hard worker, a lay minister in a Turkish city (7)
11 Battered limo leaves Kilimanjaro, set for part of Croatia (7)
12 A thousand take a short roll-on roll-off ferry back to island in the Carolines (5)
13 Language of Asia Frank translated (9)
14 Sweep a goddess off her feet: she's Greek (8)
16 Dordrecht, alternatively a German City, half in size (4)
20 Excavated road in a Madhya Pradesh city (4)
21 Danube tributary's name reflects a Chinese river and one in Georgia (8)
24 Padua jar's unusual, leading Japanese to explore here in Irian Jaya (9)
25 Trail in C Breton I leads troop of British after Columbus returns (5)
27 Portuguese city has joint support, involving one million (7)
28 With an incomplete map collection National Trust finds a Georgian city... (7)
29 ...and initially chart a part of Brazil (5)
30 Place in Bucks where the queen gets silence during the mornings (8)

Down

2 Lake in Austria Matterhorn feeds in part (5)
3 US state which is defiling Arizona? (8)
4 Sea about the Orkneys' southern head leads to a broad inlet (5,3)
5 Moor reported to a Turkish city (6)
6 Pursue almost all peripheral Native Americans to a town in Michigan... (6)
7 ...one from further down the lake, a coaching place? (9)
8 E Europeans who oddly live among crack troops (5)
9 Audibly exhort to aerate the soil in S Atlantic islands (8)
15 Capacity to absorb a song firstly in California, then a Brazilian city (9)
17 Haiti tan is not so good as one from the Pacific (8)
18 Graduate, first class, goes up to find a horse somewhere in Romania (4,4)
19 Belonging to Catalan city's not applicable, omitting a town in Portugal (8)
22 Ex-president of Pakistan gets a medic in an African country (6)
23 Chap, an American linked to this state (6)
24 Duke's account cuts back again, as in the past, Asian capital (5)
26 British and American islands in the Moluccas (5)

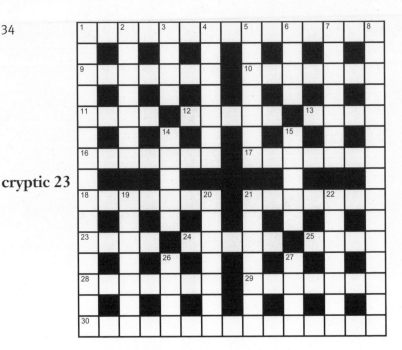

cryptic 23

Across

1 Cruelly enchaining Celts, eradicating the people (6,9)
9 Rainfall in total for S American country? (7)
10 Woods, one example of leading golfer, is set for filming north of London (7)
11 Old Russian leader reported to be in Germany (4)
12 A Mosel tester? (5)
13 Charter given to Tallinn, capital of the Baltic people? (4)
16 Airline's slow to identify a location in Sri Lanka (7)
17 ID hotel subsiding in a part of Venice (3,4)
18 Volga port railway discards, going to Kazan at first (7)
21 One from C Africa about to free king from a Roman emperor (7)
23 Depression in Ethiopia as seen from a distance (4)
24 Tiny sum of money, first hundred grand, left from someone in Europe (5)
25 State of Asia's also alarming, partly when looking back (4)
28 Throughout 11, kilometre and yards are given to a Turkish province (7)
29 Avenger's blown up a department in Macedonian Greece (7)
30 Area of Quebec's against outlay one attaches to Newfoundland, for instance (9,6)

Down

1 Absentees as I air trip to a part of the Arctic Ocean (4,8,3)
2 University of Cambridge, for example? (7)
3 Greek priestess visiting North American island from Scotland (4)
4 Copper joins medic over atmosphere rising in a part of N England (7)
5 Support the First Lady over world summit (7)
6 Bearing vessel's taken to reach a Scottish loch (4)
7 PM lost his top over Jewish character (7)
8 Correlating sand varieties here off the Nicaraguan coast (5,4,6)
14 Noisy-sounding alternative to the Malaysian rubber port? (5)
15 Asian country, derived from 'alpen'? (5)
19 Left shopper to go round Irish island (7)
20 Kick-off over article on North-South initiatives for these Asians? (7)
21 Xinjiang city church gets a new jig performed (7)
22 I'm holding glass, aiming initially for a Rio beach (7)
26 Couple left in the end for a Croatian island (4)
27 They are drained, finally entering Norfolk-Suffolk embarkation points (4)

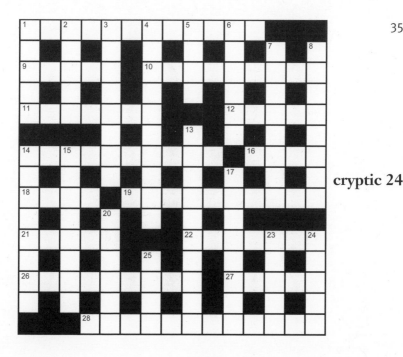

cryptic 24

Across

1 Anglican policies Japan made without the use of journal (12)
9 Georgia's borders follow a single Russian lake (5)
10 California's far-reaching coastline (4,5)
11 Brazilian state in the style of another Portuguese colony to the south (7)
12 Return one thousand at a time to city in Honshu (5)
14 Current position in the N Atlantic? (4,6)
16 Tasmanian mountain, like in the Trossachs (4)
18 Old Gascon capital given to the French Church (4)
19 Vodka rigor ruined Ukrainian city after 1991 (10)
21 Destroy a city in Tamil Nadu (5)
22 People from Selma, for example, ban 'Salaam' being used (9)
27 Hard liquor to be found around north German town (5)
28 Africans advanced to north with a Scot wearing jumpers (12)

Down

1 Portuguese city's golden avenue goes up and around (5)
2 Date popular furniture outlet ringed for Japanese motor town (5)
3 Foie gras area around Dax making mint out of slot-machines manufacturing (8)
4 Chum's characteristic knots in run between India and Sri Lanka (4,6)
5 Mozart's 36th may have been at Bruckner's place in Austria? (4)
6 Article about baron's heraldic symbol in old Britain (6)
7 Master's on vessel during Kara turbulence and an Indonesian strait (8)
8 Time to call a new date to go to the country in Asia (8)
13 Togo morass is reconstituted here in Brazil (4,6)
14 Bachelor puts on the fancy stuff in camp community on Cape Breton I (5,3)
15 One's in bed, taking after the French, at a place on the Cote d'Azur (2,6)
17 Rent and crop shortage is included to get Faeroes capital (8)
20 State of Malaysia's chaotic 25, with a thousand held standing (6)
23 24 hours of song in 'Oklahoma'? (5)
24 Timeless relative lives in old France near La Rochelle (5)
25 Unstressed sex in a Maldives paradise? (4)

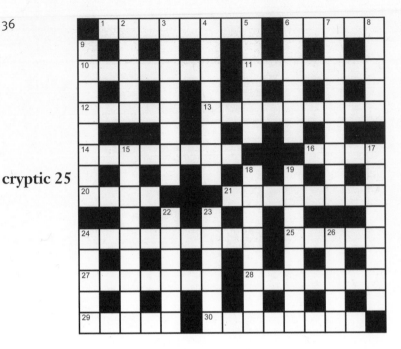

cryptic 25

Across

1 Translation of Balearic: American English it's not in this region of the Med (8)
6 They fly worker back to Algerian city (5)
10 Native American facing a charge against a half-cut Hopi (7)
11 Antrim town container following is linking initially Larne and Belfast (7)
12 Texan defence of Alabama against Missouri (5)
13 Israeli flyers this morning meet English in desert battle (2,7)
14 Part of Georgia's a bit keen, having a zone in Armenia at first (8)
16 Oxford river's noted twice (4)
20 Some anoraks usually discover a place in Xinjiang (4)
21 Half of Bosnia's capital's blown after bird trip to Serbian centre (8)
24 Italians about to go ahead of those in the north (9)
25 Ecuador's old cash is here keeping the French sweet? (5)
27 A Mailer novel, a statement of lawlessness in Wyoming's Old West? (7)
28 Honshu city's bar Middle Easterner gets round, reportedly (7)
29 Dutch regional capital's detailed submission (5)
30 Friends actress's name is included on location in Alabama (8)

Down

2 Betrayal accusation in part is hot air in France? (5)
3 Parts of Brazil, Venezuela, etc, like a strong woman to lead (8)
4 Old country in Africa where the colonialist made a first-class return? (8)
5 Part of the Alps seen from almost anywhere in France (6)
6 W African capital is a sub for construction... (6)
7 ...he rents EU building at a Swiss lake (9)
8 Wadi Mujib in Jordan, a river: not original name in Genesis? (5)
9 Japanese resort to lifting a Western Australian, Zak, about article (8)
15 A skirmish marring Asian peoples attempting to get together? (9)
17 Microwave troubles are mounting around a European country (8)
18 The haughty German and the quiet Slav? (8)
19 Chap's question involved those of the US State (8)
22 Kind of mail British soldiers put on in German port (6)
23 Exploring town in Illinois as Nebraska evacuates after storm (6)
24 Lima cocaine shrub's bound to defile in Peru... (5)
26 ...heavy coca processing is the province of Argentina (5)

cryptic 26

Across

5 Venezuelan town where it's recited, 'So long to a father, down in Demerara'? (6,7)
8 Locals say Alaskan peak study is by Arab (6)
9 Bath house in Wiltshire? (8)
10 One infiltrating ex-Iranian leader, almost is a Muslim (4)
11 Old Illyrian loan Napoli rearranged (10)
12 Record in a line extending to a city of Lorraine (6)
14 Get a fizzy drink on board airline going to somewhere in Corsica (6)
17 Place for Belizean ferry, tug 'Pandora', it turns out (5,5)
20 Greek place in Italy, in the heel, eagerly excavated (4)
21 Bavarian battle in which Churchill's at home? (8)
22 Good French wine requires vaults... (6)
23 ...let a cellar, hut perhaps, here on the Vienne (13)

Down

1 Wig worn round university; a head-covering's needed in Assam city (8)
2 Lake on the Zambezi's a joke among Kaunda extremists (6)
3 Manual used to circle a volcano in Hawaii (5,3)
4 Cardigan's style of leadership in the Crimean War? (6)
5 Here in 1993, Bohemians' independent existence was ratified? (5,8)
6 Biblical mountain where, halfway, Gilead met a serpent (6)
7 Promotion in cream teas at odd S American hot spot (7,6)
13 Place in Wales early English looked at, but only half stayed? (8)
15 Ex-Tory leader's article on Dutch admin centre (3,5)
16 Austrian falls kilometre over edge with little capacity to stop (6)
18 Friendly islander's returned, not on horseback (6)
19 Yarn nonsense originated in the Greek marketplace (6)

cryptic 27

Across

1 With rivers from Italy to England receding, Washington sits on it (7)
5 Classic race reduced to approximately ten, discovered in Dagestan city (7)
10 State of US's international position on Colombian drugs centre (4)
11 Julie so far is doubtful to reach a spot in the Hebrides (4,2,4)
12 A con in Massachusetts leads to a resort on the Costa del Sol (6)
13 Expression of disgust as French pal meets a new islander (8)
14 Student obtains academic high ground on Arthurian battle (5,4)
16 Quiet American approach to northern port in Korea (5)
17 Knock out half of old Beijing with little Russian money (5)
19 According to the Spanish the Basque Country capo's visa is forged (4,5)
23 He wrote in German, in the margin, about independence here on the Rhine (8)
24 Old part of Canada where accountant's help is rejected (6)
26 Trojan, one going back and forth to the north-east to see a French girl (10)
27 Australian's utter astonishment on getting the Ethiopian's tongue? (4)
28 French department might get the same directions as 26 (7)
29 Call one in Italian region of Veneto's capital (7)

Down

2 None died going to a conflict with a city near Tokyo (7)
3 Sanskrit derivative got from audio Riyadh put together (5)
4 A rig Hal made to reach Uttar Pradesh city (7)
6 Namibian wetland where French and Xhosa mix without getting cross (6)
7 University medic's in 11 after endless tramp to a city in Burundi (9)
8 Fleet take a northern heading to strike Indian river (7)
9 General rise in temperature's alarming GB, low after sabotage (6,7)
15 Californian resort by the Pacific littoral? (9)
18 Japanese industrial centre gets confirmation to make a Mazda's wings (7)
20 Curry, sesame one, is Thai (7)
21 Offence on a navy base means war with Russia (7)
22 Wild animal exercises on a Greek mountain in mythology (6)
25 Nurse falls in Venezuela (5)

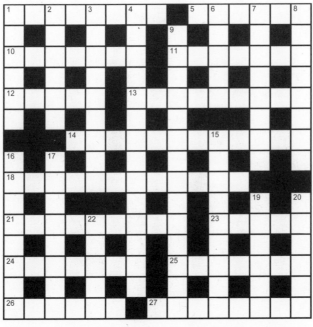

cryptic 28

Across

1 Indian city with a Bihar Reformed Church (8)
5 Chief of Old Joe's Injun braves, Wichita and Chippewa (6)
10 Guy turning round in crumpled suit gets a wave from the Japanese (7)
11 Czech city is, through glasnost, ravaged (7)
12 A pub is rejected by Shia's leader and other Semitic folk... (5)
13 ...Muslim, usually, religious a touch, almost tangent within (9)
14 Muses here before aircraft (more than half-full, going to Naxos initially) ride? (5,7)
18 Ann, an aviator, crashed here in Madagascar (12)
21 Revolutionary status is almost achieved by Soviet city (9)
23 One attempting to reach German city (5)
24 Mob gone mad in Sri Lankan tourist complex (7)
25 City of Henan where second person is inverted in an abbreviated tongue (7)
26 One of the 12, as cut off from one in the Bible (6)
27 S American capital, a United Nations offshoot, is accommodating (8)

Down

1 He dons a cape to keep out the worst elements in a Turkish city? (6)
2 German house accommodates S African and W African people (6)
3 Pole's community, after the first man on the Pitcairn Is (9)
4 Eating away at the British motorcycle base in the Cotswolds (8,6)
6 Sacking by first Saxons and Danes (5)
7 British tabloid article on Central America exposes Portuguese city (8)
8 E Africans lose odd tons to S Africans (8)
9 Orderly SAS hike is arranged for a nice part of N England (9,5)
15 Long Island retreat for Jew, almost an urban area (9)
16 US National park areas not good for anything else, perhaps? (8)
17 One gets brown playing raga here in N India... (8)
19 ...spend an hour in a pub over one Indian language (6)
20 Mineral's almost depleted state in America (6)
22 Ecstasy in turning up the last word in Greek ruins (5)

cryptic 29

Across

7 London's green hideaway's borders French, from Bois de Boulogne, perhaps (4,4)
9 A Turkish official gets recognition in finding old Dahomey capital (6)
10 Strip search for Samson here? (4)
11 101 Catholic Asians are oddly from a Russian part of the Black Sea (10)
12 Disease of the tropics? (6)
14 Ainu girl's upset one from the northern Med (8)
15 Pinnacle of the Caribbean's painting is to be seen in fitting surroundings (6)
16 Breton capital needed, little bird said (6)
19 Girl's named tree in Latin after a Michigan town (3,5)
21 Guangdong city one supports about old style hospital (6)
23 Soprano's tempo is almost at one with a Pacific atoll (10)
24 Georgia's mining gold in N Ethiopia, they say (4)
25 Greek character's heard to hesitate seeing alphabetic range in Honshu city (6)
26 French department expel poor Lee, unhealthier after failing (4-4)

Down

1 A year bringing up a sheep for a Native S American (6)
2 German affirmation, in French, in a city of old DDR (4)
3 It's crystal in France, this game (8)
4 Chap's in a British sports car going to a Javan resort (6)
5 Geezers mumbling the name of an Arkansas National Park? (3,7)
6 A realism which is changing part of Paris (2,6)
8 State of India's worker: alarming to those on the inside (6)
13 African has negotiated for these islands? (10)
15 Row over excavation by university, London's first at Tamil Nadu site... (8)
17 ...after EU family's dug up Crocodilopolis today (2,6)
18 Give weapons to one extremely girlish part of N Ireland town (6)
20 Middle Eastern trouble spot, however, not quite Ireland's internment (6)
22 Two small eastern seaboard states backed promotion in Moroccan resort (6)
24 Turkish province where there's no culture in farming (4)

cryptic 30

Across

5 Train half-empty you take from middle Himalayan peak (3,3)
7 Canadian place of low gossip, around the London area? (5,3)
9 Man's involved in several endangered species being beheaded in Indian Ocean islands (8)
10 Sailors reach American city of St Paul (6)
11 Scum the Spanish returned to France, maybe Gaul, including force to a Scottish isle (6,6)
13 City in Maharashtra where article on Hindu deity is heard (6)
15 Cell-phone centre in Alabama? (6)
18 Ancient continent's disappeared almost, need a magic wand to see Australian terrain (12)
21 Superior lake position of the French Protestant half (6)
22 Indian's capital is made while Ned fiddled (3,5)
23 Islands in the Seychelles before Muslim prince visits first (8)
24 Department, one in France to go round (6)

Down

1 Hittite capital, a marsh at first, couple of unknowns find OK during climbing (8)
2 Old Umtali's to change, they said in Rome? (6)
3 Study, over time, is a wonderful thing here in Brazil (8)
4 Tax people investigate stellar princess in Portuguese city (6)
6 Pounds UN hoards for the American nation (8)
7 Number upset by line taken by abstainers, reaching a peak in Bulgaria (6)
8 Asian river's a returning spirit (4)
12 Well known, Campbell's heel is cut ski-ing here in Scotland (4,4)
14 Pester new church over going into Sichuan city (8)
16 In France, she's in ill-humour in the sea off Quiberon (5-3)
17 Ndebele town a bit like 19, spreading endlessly, and Government intervenes (6)
18 Gym Uri set up in Armenian city (6)
19 Actor's written novel on a London borough (6)
20 A fool turning round to visit a Pacific island (4)

cryptic 31

Across

7 One walks out of biblical land, reaching a point on the Volga (6)
8 Girl's name, accepted in the Pacific islands (8)
9 Funny Asian lot, these inhabitants of old Indo-China (8)
10 Little in weight, has a heroin cargo to land in Antarctica (6)
11 Unmake aa formations which identify Hawaiian volcano? (5,3)
12 Chap gets a first-class return to N Ossetia (6)
13 Alpaca Ann organized this morning in a Pacific to Atlantic excavation (6,5)
18 Communist country place one American in a Brazilian city (6)
20 Dodgy corned beef Foreign Office naughtily export to somewhere in Hungary (8)
22 Russian lake boy's associated with, going back in the past (6)
23 Male group's nickname in a Congo river port (8)
24 Poor chaperon gets a tip in America (4,4)
25 Eclipse is visible from a Californian city (6)

Down

1 Blast back at a pub on India's west coast (7)
2 Georgia's the girl in N Carolina town... (8)
3 ...a new bird's parading around one in Scotland (6)
4 Brazilian river's air is filled with water, as they say in Portuguese (8)
5 Veto a student visiting an island in Kiribati (6)
6 Taka Ali split in a Syrian port (7)
8 USA commandant placed in a part of Arabia until 1970 (6,3,4)
14 Native Americans quietly leaving Cyprus resort after a censure (8)
15 African's going to live in a road around the highlands in Kenya (8)
16 India state Guangzhou's extreme position over vessel is a tad touchy... (7)
17 ...and German support for border potassium found by Uttar Pradesh lake (7)
19 Amateur finds the beginning of zinc deposits here in the Atlantic (6)
21 The French 'breadbasket', a handsome one to the Church? (6)

cryptic 32

Across

1 Capital for New Caledonia and Oman EU transferred (6)
5 Revolutions restrict modern Greek tourist islands (8)
9 Rhine city run by new chap, squeezing drugs (8)
10 Crazy machos battle for Hungarian town? (6)
11 European treaty, with wealthy among the abstainers, on Dutch river (10)
12 Czech city's comes after a navy's first officer (4)
13 American in new pursuit of a goddess (8)
16 Germany's quiet withdrawal from partial occupation here in the east (6)
17 Aloft, transporting one east to a part of Greece near 28 (6)
19 Old Testament Ark, aka explosion waiting to happen in Victorian times? (8)
21 Rejection of Christmas in part of Mexico (4)
22 Meet Zambian web of intrigue crossing this border (10)
25 Extreme part of Australia where British genus of lizard is reared (6)
26 A Greek character seen a yard or so from Asian river (3,5)
27 Marines spread out, exploring waters around the Moluccas (5,3)
28 Classical city which was then as new? (6)

Down

2 A plant established in the environs of a city in the Pakistani Punjab... (5)
3 ...Rajasthani people employed in vitamin assignments (5)
4 French department almost replicates Australian lake in flower (7)
5 Lure a hundred into old European Economic Community? (7)
6 Scottish cairns where saint is found in an open-ended chamber (7)
7 A graduate in various chats with a supplier of water in Canada (9)
8 Directions to defraud the Queen when in Californian city (9)
14 French feature's not about a British pantomime character (5,4)
15 One troubled 24 to obtain independent German affirmation in old Papua Barat (5,4)
18 Horrendous hazards for Georgian muslims (7)
19 Capital in Africa to install power in half the desert (7)
20 Water like in 27 Australian Air Force poured on mountains endlessly (7)
23 Kind of resentment to a cape Scots have (5)
24 Caucasian's primarily athletic, robust, young and Nazi (5)

cryptic 33

Across

8 One from Honshu goes quietly, replaced by five of another island (8)
9 A wheat processing town in Uttar Pradesh (6)
10 Area of Normandy to rear pony to a certain span (6)
11 All points to tea date at Byron's pile in Notts (8)
12 Alas, poor me, sounding hesitant at Holland's largest flower auction (8)
13 Caribbean island's the place to shoot duck (6)
14 Ignoramus Oz, Stan, gets disorientated in the Iranian highlands (6,9)
18 Girl bumped into Aboriginals in central Australia (6)
20 A bleak period in America: number the Indian tribes relocated here? (8)
23 Welsh town a girl hits during troubled comeback (8)
24 Gross Russian officiousness zoning, naming Yeltsin, first in Chechnya? (6)
25 Restrict to a smallish number, 8, bantams from here originally (6)
26 Following church elder, Royal Marine evacuated people from an old part of Iraq (8)

Down

1 Pub making a fuss turning up in the former princely state of India (6)
2 Many get drunk, arak going around a ship in old Ujung Pandang (8)
3 Unbelievably meek, the French capital in Tigré (6)
4 He designed aircraft landing here in Rome (8,2,5)
5 Part of Nunavut previously Ken Waite explored (8)
6 Bill is able to go up to Cambridge, shortly (6)
7 Uzbek city's set-up run by a newly-formed gang (8)
15 Place in the Auvergne to find gold by a stream, beneath Cevennes' summit (8)
16 State imperialist Russia maybe disputed: part of Germany now (8)
17 Snake rises here in Montana? (8)
19 Samoyeds of the north have no head for principles (6)
21 Hound an Asian (6)
22 Spectacles fall from Aussie's jumper in a Malaysian border town (6)

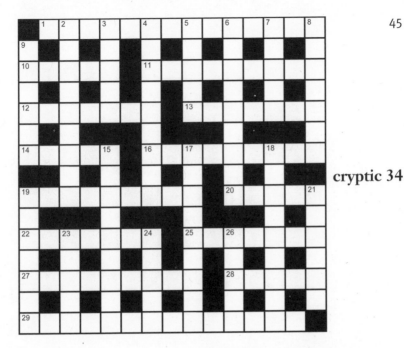

cryptic 34

Across

1 R Darling fens, pouring out east and south of Australian mountains? (8,6)
10 The Spanish guerrilla region? (5)
11 Bahamian island before the time detective after drugs is beheaded (9)
12 Austrian town's church is after a Roman building (7)
13 Cook in Aotearoa discovered fruit, nearly all in first-class packaging (7)
14 Revolutionary French valley town! (5)
16 Old Arabian ate banana messily (9)
19 Ditch American with two grand in eastern Turkish province (9)
20 About 56 seen at a Corsican resort, which also took Nelson's eye? (5)
22 Rift forcing first Catholics out of, and one thousand into, religion (7)
25 Norseman is being held by a city in Thessaly (7)
27 A light reading and a strong drink in a city of Honshu (9)
28 Tanzanian town's award, a year early (5)
29 In French, does she say her sleeve's in the drink? Translate! (7,7)

Down

2 Hell coven frolicking in Scottish water (4,5)
3 New Zealand, for instance, is linked to a Tanzanian town (5)
4 A symbol of India in front of Mumbai harbour (9)
5 Three points one can enter a place in Italy (5)
6 Polar cart used in caper (9)
7 Environmentalist at one with a tributary of the Colorado? (5)
8 Yemeni, perhaps? No, Arkansas German, from Augsburg in the old days (7)
9 Years later reside back, creating a round, in Somerset town (6)
15 Finnish water reservoir one gets to Middle East location another way (4,5)
17 Lived the life of Vivien, for example, in a rum place in Queensland (9)
18 Island port on Merseyside (9)
19 Avalanche in the West Coast range (7)
21 Scot gets ill in a Nigerian city (6)
23 Island in the Gulf's with Kazakh/Argentinean interests (5)
24 Irish county money, where Erica's head comes from (5)
26 Paul's detailed letter describing the Empire (5)

cryptic 35

Across
8 Through Christmas, a danger, as Jews were besieged here (6)
9 Strict vegetarian restricted girl going around US fun city (3,5)
10 Is seen in Pennsylvania and a Tuscan city (4)
11 Eats gammon messily at an Algerian port (10)
12 Place in Italy, lost north of 2, and heard to hesitate to the west (6)
14 Shot a deserter in a Victorian gold town (8)
15 Poor Darfur doctor, separated and abandoned, gets to Turkish city (4)
16 Eastern spice arriving at French lagoon (5)
18 Extreme southern part of Iran (4)
19 Throw most of the weight behind the monarch here in Jamaica (8)
22 Treaty with French ally in French school here in the north of the country (6)
23 Kind of wave heading NE to Thailand is curtailed in a part of Pacific (10)
25 17 alternatively called by some quarter Ashanti, for instance (4)
27 Stupidly ran out of Ulan Bator wanting to hide route to an African city (8)
28 Tributary of the Tagus, one 16 where nothing runs off (6)

Down
1 Party man first to last in Ulster (4)
2 Support one in holding up a French water transport over in S Italy (8)
3 Tree-bedecked valley somewhere in California (8)
4 Greek ruins, initially Egyptian, lost in Santorini (4)
5 Setback: part of a clear single-mindedness of this country? (6)
6 Secure by rope, reaching a tributary of the Volga (6)
7 Rift valley feature, eventually point out, is about Kenya's yen to break free (4,6)
13 Island drink that French adopted (10)
14 Take a direction which leads to a part of the French Pyrenees (5)
17 Deplorably hang a number after one Australian and an African (8)
18 In India, old Oudh capital's a poor base against revolutionary Zia force (8)
20 European material English ignored (6)
21 A name given to Chinese society by a Pacific islander (6)
24 Tax passed by Edinburgh Parliament? (4)
26 Golden account on Portuguese mountains (4)

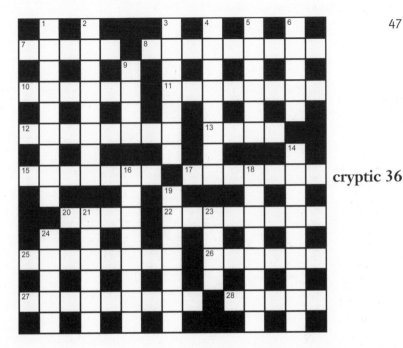

cryptic 36

Across

7 Barbadian's first month after getting a degree (5)
8 Ban guava production, a year behind here in Quebec (6,3)
10 Texan town the French build again (6)
11 Emperor closed off borders, an automatic reaction in part of the Med (8)
12 On Kenya's borders where British fliers cover a stage to the falls (8)
13 Place in Xinjiang thousands in gold (4)
15 Indonesian article read last and carried (7)
17 Ancient Mexican pot found in ruins on the Yucatan (7)
20 The thing to do in an English spa town? (4)
22 Old British PM is able when in Palma (8)
25 Pet's a hit in a Peloponnesian resort (8)
26 Might be getting ticket to return to Israeli resort (3,3)
27 Ankara aim is to transform a former Armenian state (9)
28 Sounds like a sweet spot in Sri Lanka (5)

Down

1 Southern girls, with adult, quiet since in the Pacific islands (9)
2 Indian city chap finds going south, Goa by name (8)
3 Nearly half of Israeli port blown away after girl arrives at Iraqi city (2,5)
4 Corrupt laird has mother restricted, subjected to a Pictish kingdom (8)
5 155' canoes lose knots, heading, now depth (6)
6 People of the sea cut out this vegetable (5)
9 One extracted Idahoan capital to find a city in Guangxi (4)
14 Basque city pub, and a cold beer nearly full to party with (9)
16 Remains of a fire as early Tatars return to sack falling Turkmen capital (8)
18 Indian city amir ransacked with emperor (8)
19 They say in Ethiopia this morning, retrospectively Gershwin's featured in church (7)
21 Place in Turkey to dry off for Noah? (6)
23 African river in the mountains: as in France, river splits before entering bay (4)
24 Native American turned round, leaving one from Indonesia (5)

cryptic 37

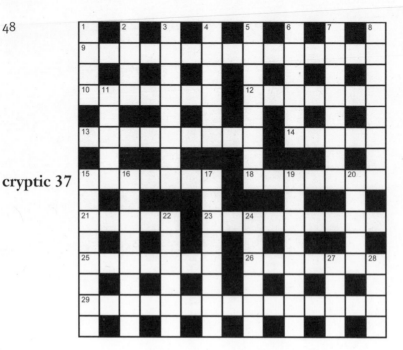

Across

9 Gold maybe by moor in US beauty spot (11,4)
10 Caravan by wadi crashed, one taken to a town in Madhya Pradesh (7)
12 Goddess at home in the West and the Mid West state (7)
13 Old land in the Caucasus in terrible crisis about being involved in the Azeri front (9)
14 Texas town plot by a roundabout (5)
15 Number in Georgia, eleven, go to an autonomous part of China (7)
18 Lake in Asia, as real as a mirage – as not! (4,3)
21 Reportedly pollute and make smaller a Cameroonian national park (5)
23 Lake District town I had eaten at first, after walks (9)
25 Cool part of Czech Republic? (7)
26 Bahamian island's thousand-to-nothing return opens accounts (7)
29 Aberrant, nasty, dubious characters hide silver somewhere in Rhode I (12,3)

Down

1 Oriental kind of ox found in Alaskan ski resort (4)
2 Scots for Scotland? Argument at first weighted against Anglos' leader? (4)
3 Love the way fashionable types imbibe French wine (8)
4 A Welsh girl's with continentals (6)
5 Get Honshu city or Yakima in quiz (8)
6 English hills get lower after an endless run up (6)
7 Article incorporated new 4s and old 4s (8)
8 Musical state in the US (8)
11 I get into headgear I needed for the Caribbean country (5)
15 Crosby, after New York knock-out, hits Danish city (8)
16 Part of Ireland to find Hornet training with the navy (8)
17 American, a bachelor after a large retainer (8)
19 US President informally happy to state detailed capital for Nigeria's Ogun (8)
20 Study after yours truly returned to a German port (5)
22 Girl's father is in Argentina, it's plain (6)
24 Siberian city where Kelvin chases after spoiled kids (6)
27 Some big boys among Nigerians (4)
28 Reported snags crossing to the other side, according to the Greeks (4)

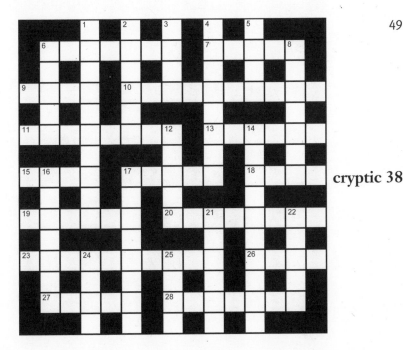

cryptic 38

Across

6 Chop and change course to a city of Orissa (7)
7 Mere sound evokes this haven in Dorset... (5)
9 ...less idyllic-sounding is a sickly Hubei city! (4)
10 England, No 1 corrupt nation, like 20 and another island (3-7)
11 Turkish province, one time in a part of the British Empire (8)
13 African people are at home in a boat... (6)
15 Excuse one deserting to a city of the Midi (4)
17 Heights of success Israelis experienced in 1967 and 1973? (5)
18 Obtained top hurdler, one from a German race (4)
19 Move to Madrid to start with, then a time on one of the Canaries (6)
20 Caribbean island train did crash... (8)
23 ...in 1902; an explosion is heard on Martinique? (5,5)
26 American oil's backing to cordon off Chinese river (4)
27 Capital for Tigré in the past went via Xanadu way (5)
28 Obtain almost all dye going to a place of torment in Israel (7)

Down

1 Let Italian unravel what separates the Turks and Greeks on Cyprus... (6,4)
2 ...he supports limited answer England-New Zealand put up here in Emilia-Romagna (6)
3 W African girl nearly gets away from American (4)
4 Wisconsin city fruit's not processed (8)
5 Northern peninsula 26 abandon for S Chinese people (4)
6 S American leaves European mountains to find Andean flower (5)
8 Port of Washington's always tee total, after a point (7)
12 A last adjustment's in place in Belgium (5)
14 A new measure university's taken's a small solution for W Indians (10)
16 Peruvian mining centre railway enters into a loo arrangement, the first in Andes... (2,5)
17 ...a little weight one's put in the pan in the mountains? (8)
21 Nigerian city that's hot, oddly, around low southern area (6)
22 Turn up the degrees penetrating lava, as in Hawaii, in a Honshu volcano (5)
24 Sound haven for Greenland capital (4)
25 Carry to old Galician city (4)

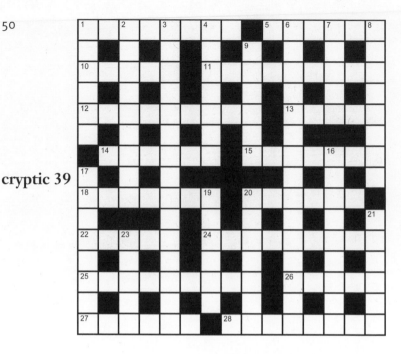

cryptic 39

Across

1 Scale of the wind in a part of the Arctic Ocean (8)
5 The French lads take a year out to go to an island of women... (6)
10 ...even gold is given to remain here in France (5)
11 Outrageous wag, Ronnie Wood, according to Lennon up north? (9)
12 Mesa pueblo's a commune built on American music (5,4)
13 Chinese family's old island place in Vietnam (5)
14 Rule applied to new Oklahoman town (6)
15 Number leading attack against New York mob beheaded in Chinatown? (7)
18 Oriental holiday destination (7)
20 Supporters have little weight to carry back to a Texan river (6)
22 Surprising interjection, in a vow to reach US state (5)
24 Dogs sound more coy, say, in wood-lined English county? (9)
25 Drink acceptable to a fallen saint here in the Pacific (9)
26 French pal joins quiet Christian sect (5)
27 Ecuadorean community on island, a Scottish island (6)
28 Iraqi Gnostic made naan properly (8)

Down

1 Balkan's hiding in Istanbul garden (6)
2 Nazi arson involved specific Americans (9)
3 Get one to treat people near Perth for wind (9,6)
4 Organized thug with capital from Myanmar (7)
6 A thick skinned type (perhaps Australian?) is to dock somewhere in Mumbai harbour (9,6)
7 One vegetable grows around a city in Heilongjiang Province (5)
8 National Theatre-Shakespeare character raised South American capital (8)
9 Ankara's failure to see the state of Burma (6)
16 Australian's beginning in Lincoln (9)
17 Resort to Baja California after Arab state becomes limited (8)
19 From a part of Sudan, point to an Independent getting ahead (6)
20 See the sea, with the sound of sheep all about, in a valley in S Australia (7)
21 Sichuan city where family from 13 put up the French (6)
23 Native American's a supporter of the old British protectorate (5)

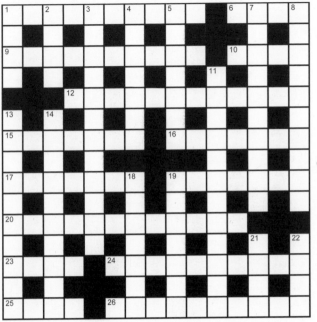

cryptic 40

Across

1 Gateaus can be messy in this part of Costa Rica (10)
6 Graduate officer from Estonia, perhaps (4)
9 Swedish port captures Icelandic money (10)
10 Get beer by the yard in this US university (4)
12 Jog Ankara's position as currency from 9 opens ski resort in Slovenia (8,4)
15 Underworld opening near Naples? (7)
16 Rhodes summit, primarily a time to cut Egyptian capital at source (7)
17 Shooter fires, but not loudly, in a Turkish city (7)
19 Uruguay resort to money from 1a with a first-class return (7)
20 Misdirected aerogramme about British university to a passionate place in Bavaria? (12)
23 Loan used old French capital (4)
24 Endless month in French zone for DEA, ringing Brazilian city (4,2,4)
25 Irish water navy entered previously (4)
26 What waves may do to kings? They need fins by the sound of it (10)

Down

1 Treasure a Normandy beach (4)
2 A river on strange course in Tuscany (4)
3 Eurasians not involved in this language group? (12)
4 Directions after weekend in Irish islands, for Icelandic port (7)
5 Round fish is one to land in the Med (7)
7 S Americans surprise Greeks islanders: that's a turn up, and wrong? (10)
8 Article bringing North and South together in the States? (3,7)
11 Actors sick on beer getting round northern part of Spain (8-4)
13 Looker Gail is wasted in Aussie outback town (10)
14 Telemann week in school place near Washington (10)
18 Uranium in mountain chap found climbing somewhere in Mozambique (7)
19 Reef around Australia popular in Belizean border town (7)
21 Old Algerian port's skeletal remains (4)
22 A section to master on Dutch river (4)

cryptic 41

Across

7 Antipodean the French turned back and banned from being a European (8)
8 Brazil state piece of writing doesn't need accompanying drawing (4)
9 Age bones which evolve into a C African of the present (8)
10 A man rounds a point to discover the longest river W of the Andes (6)
11 Spoil that's left accounts for state of the Volga east of Moscow (4,2)
12 One into home improvement's an ace in part of Turkey (8)
13 Tamil, another minority section of Italian city, so Italians say (6)
14 Distributed EU glut to people in Andhra Pradesh (6)
16 Training place for the RAF Charlie organized efficiently (8)
19 One from a northern state makes a final attempt for a Hindi India (6)
21 Directions given to dock in SW France (6)
22 S American secretary's put forward a study on a Californian city (8)
23 People in the Balkans once linked to a French department (4)
24 Part of Gascony drink to Magna Carta? No thanks, it's not right (8)

Down

1 Nicaraguan department's Handel oratorio is sounding almost right (6)
2 Escape from computer exam about one to get to Philip's old place in Spain (8)
3 Friends of the Earth from the Arctic? (12)
4 Dull over a period of time in Italy's Basilicata region (6)
5 Country ditched the peso with injection of money – Bahrain capital (6)
6 Part of Aotearoa where a bloke gets over women at university (8)
10 British old money, primarily, is second to gold in W African country (6-6)
13 Harbours Australian in the Pacific islands (8)
15 Sudan nag organization to expose E Africans (8)
17 Gujarati city where Poona Diadem is carried (6)
18 Lounge in peace around Rhodes island, being the first to the Mediterranean archipelago (6)
20 Heads from French city, taking in bearings for somewhere in the Alps (6)

cryptic 42

Across

7 No 3rd dan karate characters found in W African city (5)
8 Kodiak, maybe, makes a Canadian lake (5,4)
10 Language of Indonesia's a Sabah hybrid (6)
11 Brandy firm's dropped after first-class rugby's return in a prehistoric French town (8)
12 Chap seen among jazz types, maybe Barcelona folk (8)
13 Native Americans' university receives setback (4)
15 Sheep-rearing, to a degree, at Livingstone's place in Zambia today (7)
17 Unlocked number of the French occupiers in Guadalquivir town (7)
20 Should this magazine recognize a part of Morocco since 1969? (4)
22 Retire petroleum king in Persia to a location on Crete (8)
25 Portuguese point to W Europe's extreme position (4,4)
26 It's found in several pinewoods of the European uplands (6)
27 Part of Ireland under the English spell, where the Tory's given nothing in the past? (9)
28 Oddly, two alternatively sitting in a river in Portugal (5)

Down

1 Old Asian country mutton? Not quite how they say it in Kerala (9)
2 Turn up, Gamay being found at a temperature near a Honshu city (8)
3 A number roped into British Railways' weekend to Russian city (7)
4 An Air UK schedule carries ring to a Tunisian holy site (8)
5 Colombian city where I capture EU phoney (6)
6 Initially beat and torture and kill N Sumatran ethnic group (5)
9 Sound of sheep around lake, somewhere in Wales... (4)
14 ...around 'lac', in posing Queensland resort (9)
16 Kazakh coal-mining city where Russians found space? (8)
18 Every German boat capsized, on the water making for a Scottish port (8)
19 Attack a character from Greece in Japanese city (7)
21 Foreign Office's circumvention in the matter of Poles in a Californian city (6)
23 A British vintage motorcycle turned up around a Kalahari settlement (4)
24 The fatty-type, even, goes over the top in this Greek island (5)

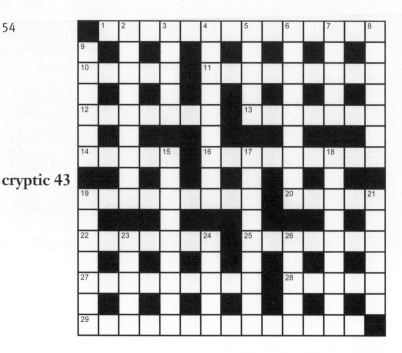

cryptic 43

Across

1 Daunt anarchist uprising in Atlantic isle (7,2,5)
10 Entry to Britain needs the date on top (5)
11 When all at sea, Argonauts get bitter (9)
12 New lot of boats seen in sacred Indian river (7)
13 Mountains detailed after Australian Air Force reach the sea (7)
14 Hawaiian greeting's stressed a little differently in a Scottish town? (5)
16 He plays the piano for a Polish Jew (9)
19 The W Indian soldier, not one a Royal Scot (9)
20 A graduate gets a question on a Jordanian port (5)
22 Town in Upper Silesia exchanged rotas with Virginia (7)
25 Sea air improves around the start of Urals, in this place of two continents (7)
27 Almost fancy I'm a gunner in a Portuguese city (9)
28 About US money being halved: not applicable to a Zambian mining centre (5)
29 Answer to rest? Unanimous when rambling in a part of the Sahara Atlas (5,9)

Down

2 Relieve British Rail in shambles it runs in Germany (5,4)
3 Asian country has dealings in messy rials (5)
4 A ruin avatar, not a deity, turned up at a Buddhist stupa in India (9)
5 Excavation by Yoruba's bordering on Ghanaian national park (5)
6 Price a Mexican table in a Californian city (5,4)
7 Pacific island, first unaccountably regulated under Australia, naturally needed to turn this round? (5)
8 Pre-Pueblo culture around southern America is a kind of national socialism (7)
9 Polish city send number to 5's excavation (6)
15 Were Algonquins sometimes derogatorily called rednecks here? (9)
17 Herons meet end tragically in a Pacific island run by 18... (9)
18 ...man's first settlement on a Christian Pitcairn? (9)
19 Excited, even anger pervades, in the taking back of a Caucasian state (7)
21 Sounds like Swedish group may be able to find Khakassian city... (6)
23 ...German city Romans built is discovered by one who is persistent (5)
24 A firm hand needed at the bow to find Bahamian islands (5)
26 Retrospective in Radnorshire, partly for an Andalusian town (5)

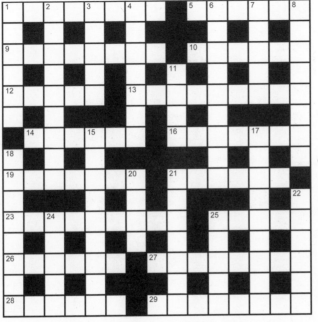

cryptic 44

Across
1 Knock out road to circle supporter of Sudan's centre (8)
5 US agents turn back after a junior officer's form of language in C Asia (6)
9 Actor and screenwriter seen together in a Tunisian resort (8)
10 Quebec peninsula two E Coast states named, following United Nations lead (6)
12 Track in Italy bird extinct around Aotearoa (5)
13 Analysand exploited African country before 1964? (9)
14 Boys from Bridgetown in bars is OK in Germany (6)
16 Allow British multi-national a place up the Amazon (7)
19 Old Dordogne caves discovered after the Spanish note to the French (7)
21 Abandoned hysteria uncommon in Salisbury of old (6)
23 Tricky landing this morning in a marshy part of Botswana... (9)
25 ...for a part somewhat like mine in the Kalahari (5)
26 A wheat processing town in Uttar Pradesh (6)
27 Italian, one from 12, maybe a long way outside a northern place, finally (8)
28 Out-of-date meat found near Manchester (6)
29 Place for Japanese engineering perhaps accommodated in 12 in the old days? (8)

Down
1 Ring man in Kerala being evacuated to a place in Nagaland (6)
2 Asian seen in central Graz with Poles and other Europeans (9)
3 Tomahawk strike: tense week for US Strategic Air Command (5)
4 American, after defacing pub, gets the beginning of Hell here in Italy (7)
6 House that ruled it bombed Germany (9)
7 A master South African climbed a peak in Japan (5)
8 Handel composed about a hundred, primarily of the Old Testament type (8)
11 Place in Dublin initially determining all Irish legislation (4)
15 AA whisk Australian away, first to get drunk at saké-brewing place in Japan (9)
17 Historic Spanish city with a Gascon town featured in a classic map (9)
18 Drink north of the river defines this part of S Portugal (8)
20 A new team promoted to find terracotta soldiers here in China (4)
21 Dido he abandoned at a Yemeni port (7)
22 River stopped winding after Kali's top half is seen over the Cauvery (6)
24 A nation of Finns? (5)
25 Address headgear required at a place on the northern tip of Honshu (5)

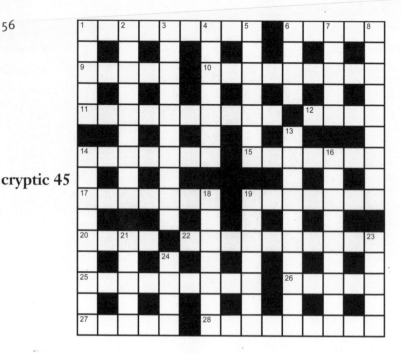

cryptic 45

Across

1 A vile aim, dastardly ambushing individual on 9 road in Italy (3,6)
6 Native Americans, ancient fellows both, almost 100 (5)
9 Italian letters to be learned from 20? (5)
10 One of the faithful, he settled in Pitcairn I (9)
11 Glider navigator's instructions on seeing market garden operation in Australia? (6,4)
12 Port from near Oporto's robust, not sour, liquid (4)
14 Woman's house name is after a girl from Boise, perhaps (7)
15 There's anger over the country when it comes to the state of Europe (7)
17 Europe's a sea of Basque mutterings (7)
19 Hag Adam toured with in an ancient Indian kingdom (7)
20 It's as easy as this to get a date in some Brazilian cities (4)
22 Defiles bird trapped in a Scottish resort (10)
25 Execute a little boy before returning to Bihari city (9)
26 Raise new crops up in a region in S Chile (5)
27 Sign of a pause in sentencing somewhere in Panama? (5)
28 Turkish place has promotion to get rare La Paz air, leaving second class (9)

Down

1 A fleet based in Virginia's making for Bulgarian port... (5)
2 ...American marines insane to negotiate for those cut off from the Black Sea? (9)
3 I classically get trapped between 19d, mostly, and sea resort in Jamaica (7,3)
4 Note church domain is curtailed by a river in Australia (7)
5 The first Iranian to produce angora on a mountain in Aotearoa? (7)
6 French department which gets the pick of the framboises? (4)
7 British car about to dock in Rio Muni (5)
8 Agreement for an Argentinian port on Uruguay river? (9)
13 Novel car from Ford in Spanish S America in the past called the Conquistador? (3,7)
14 Icicle Dan produced, being Norse (9)
16 Shoe, peep-toed little number in America, reaches the south of Spain (9)
18 Ocean where one hundred are lost near a point in Georgia... (7)
19 ...a mass is held, but sounds like you and I must leave the state... (7)
21 ...about to test the sea again? (5)
23 A mid-air lapse at first makes Egyptian desert (5)
24 Burmese hills country area that's deprived (4)

cryptic 46

Across

8 Destination in Rio Muni found when turning a label round (4)
9 Rake up poor soil in a semi-arid area of S Africa (5,5)
10 Romanian port extravaganza attracts less than a fair portion of glitz (6)
11 Almost trap con man one follows on patch in Sardinia (8)
12 Part of India, horse country which includes Assam to the west? (8)
14 CIA in a station cut off here in the Bahamas (6)
16 Kyushu port put the first oil into tankers accidentally... (4)
17 ...it has a sobriquet circulating a port in Honshu (5)
18 Where William the Conqueror lived is a lavatory English built inside (4)
19 Number attracted to Swedish university place from New Caledonia (6)
21 He led French troops behind a wood to an island in the Channel (8)
23 Old Mexican, the first hidalgo accepted into a form of Buddhism (8)
26 Carpet capital of Wiltshire in the past? (6)
27 Questions US ask here in Cuba, it being not Managua for a change (10)
28 It's a Turkish province, and out of place in the north (4)

Down

1 Brazilian state to spoil Nigerian capital for Surinam (10)
2 Samoan protection against repeated volcanic outpourings? (4-4)
3 Apt to be controversial, putting American zone in Hungary, it's plain (6)
4 Initially the price of global warming? (4)
5 Gaia aura's strange to see in a tributary of the Tocantins (8)
6 Thanks a chap from Rome in reaching the Algarve resort (6)
7 Old S African after the matter of the Siberian river trip (4)
13 Adult swallow nearly lands on a watercourse in the Balkans (5)
15 Acceptable to all sides, English wetland's the key to eastern Georgian swamp (10)
17 Syrian leader gets heard at a poor Iranian city (8)
18 Chap left in charge of letters from Russia (8)
20 Makes money on old Kincardineshire's name (6)
22 Not right what a graffitist does to historic city of the Yukon? (6)
24 City of the Dominican Rep's made up of Africans, with 50% of one people being enslaved (4)
25 Silver and gold in an Ethiopian Cushitic dialect (4)

cryptic 47

Across

1 Shattered, Jimi Hendrix cancelled most of second half in a Honshu city (6)
4 Old Indians, masters about bringing a deserter to the Hindu leader (8)
10 Nine, almost Force Eleven, reaching a remote part of China (7)
11 A British car, without royal support, in move to Bulgarian city (7)
12 Sort of turn at Tahoe, with nothing to the east, to get out of the state (4)
13 NHS, being poor, left humanitarians to deal with African country (10)
15 Belgian canal, one of the Victorian era? (6)
16 Conserve aid mostly California's given to a Caribbean island (7)
20 A number of the French reject British rule in Andalucian town (7)
21 Greek port's a knack of retreating into the Greek character (6)
24 Agra gang an evil presence here on the Pakistani border (10)
26 Pigmeat accepted (or pig iron?) in Syrian steel town (4)
28 Small Asian, for instance, in Niort, travelling (7)
29 Inter last lost king in a country near 13 (7)
30 Greek city's name, after a goddess put on a happy face (8)
31 American country girl put the tin hat on it (6)

Down

1 Titled, famous old boxer, one from C America? (8)
2 Place on the Tarn where boatman took in a bend and turned north (9)
3 Jack gets nine-to-one to find a city in Heilongjiang (4)
5 Swedish water may irritate and chap (8)
6 Tunic of a friar maybe not right in a Pakistani city (10)
7 On Ijsselmeer, is it Dutch hoe, but not quite, or a pole? (5)
8 Doesn't sound too efficient, this little cleaner from E Europe (6)
9 One in the NW Frontier's hot from a Buddhist centre near Kathmandu (5)
14 Original Chilean monkey-puzzle tree's right away from new, planted in the north... (10)
17 ...after a century at Arica: CIA developed to take to site NW of Vitória in Brazil (9)
18 Cards involving a quiet circle here in the Peruvian foothills of the Andes... (8)
19 ...range of mountains: welcome's extended to an Asian and American (8)
22 Positive in Russia after lake shores disappear in a part of Africa (6)
23 Sumatran city make a spread with a vitamin additive (5)
25 Move 28 to/from country near 29? (5)
27 Intellectual pursuit American supported in a Greek city (4)

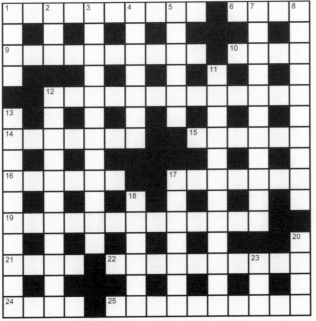

cryptic 48

Across

1 Genial wags, crude and Scottish (10)
6 Sanctimonious self-help group seen around Samoan capital (4)
9 Gold ring in the past a poor link to Mogul capital (10)
10 Centre of 6's island off Northumberland (4)
12 Met NHS analyst going round the regal Lancashire links (6,2,5)
14 European country, one rebutting return into a changing East (7)
15 Resort in Mexico from putting tin before copper, and initially nickel (6)
16 Africans open Greek letters in an uprising (3,3)
17 Turned up in a panama hat, allowing for hot and cold changes in the desert (7)
19 Sandiness in LA is due to a shift in a Pacific archipelago (6,7)
21 Exhortation to boycott Scottish port (4)
22 Ravenous GI is lost describing a part of the Central Massif in France (10)
24 Head for a Scottish loch (4)
25 WWII battle is short, with Germans reportedly against E Europeans (10)

Down

1 Holding a fool over fighting here in the Pacific (4)
2 Take a short time to discover a German wine valley (3)
3 N Carolina town where Churchill's drink's made initially (7-5)
4 Seat, established in S Spain, makes this car model? (7)
5 A vessel is seen in a Western Australian rift valley lake (6)
7 Ancient Mediterraneans, one Hispanic, getting involved (11)
8 5 was this East African chasm where Indian died out (10)
11 Bag a narwhal? A far-fetched situation inland in the Pakistani Punjab (12)
12 14's near neighbours illuminated, in the grip of the Germans, anti-aircraft positioning around Ulster... (11)
13 ...and Munster, perhaps? It may be replicated here in Ohio (10)
17 Pass in Austria beer with gravity, odd recipe British imported (7)
18 16 African grasses not seen, of course, in 12a? (6)
20 In Oxford, there's a course, one with little relative support... (4)
23 ...not one jot, leaving one Japanese place (3)

cryptic 49

Across

7 Nice place in LA to call home (3,3)
8 Hasid AGM arranged for an oasis in the Sahara (8)
9 Cypriots resort to refurbishing mill to house a craft circle (8)
10 Name given to beer pub in a Dutch Rhine town (6)
11 Peruvian city's smart design without getting extremely upbeat (8)
12 Massive steel complex in Liaoning's a direction to steer away from (6)
13 Foot playing up? It's pronounced when reaching a place near Lucknow (11)
18 Malaysian port rejecting a kind of cabbage at the beginning of May (6)
20 Fish making a positive comeback to island off Wales (8)
22 One who's into the habit of scaling a point in Cornwall? (6)
23 French wine to induce slash serial killer to come round (8)
24 Rent about almost all of Riviera resort and a place just on the outskirts (2,6)
25 Name first of pip-less fruits after a place in Italy (6)

Down

1 Rebel top guns pulled out of housing project being built in a West Bank town (7)
2 Quixotic chap's part of Spain? (2,6)
3 State of India is encapsulated in Doris' sacrifice (6)
4 Western pseudonym might be taken up at Academy in Honshu city (8)
5 Brazilian's city's gay, so it's sent up (6)
6 Quote given to the French abbey in 23 (7)
8 Fought flab: a km run north of Mumbai, in the main (4,2,7)
14 Something magical managed without spades for peoples of Africa (8)
15 Gag region around an Andean oasis (8)
16 Plots rumoured in a Wiltshire market town... (7)
17 ...and evidence of drug-taking here on the Isle of Wight? (7)
19 A malicious article exposes Iranian port (6)
21 Place in Catalonia eastern lad incarcerated in Georgia (6)

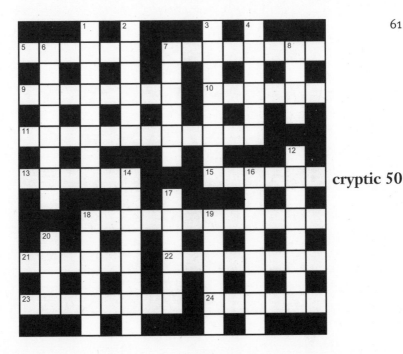

cryptic 50

Across

5 Gang from Uganda's in alcoholic haze when colonel sadly departs (6)
7 African swamp where it's all right for a vehicle to proceed (8)
9 At first, doing Russia: Odessa's under zero; healthier by active Black Sea resort (8)
10 Travel back to the north-east and north-west part of Turkey (6)
11 Landmark in Massachusetts when W Country music is introduced there? (8,4)
13 Eggs on senior officer here, as they say in Italy (6)
15 Czech and Denmark's borders? Cross close to German river (6)
18 Pub managed by a writer on the front in a Colombian port (12)
21 About time 20 find cold water in N Europe... (6)
22 ...from these islands, foresee a maelstrom (8)
23 Hubei city team angers half the supporter backing (8)
24 Devon city's secret executive is, in part, a throwback (6)

Down

1 Putting a band round how in Latin American port? (8)
2 Greek character a number in Rome hush over one of the gods (6)
3 Where in S Africa to shelter a loved one during scare to the north (4,4)
4 Place in the Scottish borders is hard to find with a bit of a candle (6)
6 Aluminium and sulphur discovered in a vital area of the Pacific (5,3)
7 Address machine in Kansas City's lack of capital? (6)
8 Former Portuguese enclave without a name deserted by the Indian people (4)
12 Man maybe is following boy to somewhere in N England (8)
14 Landing in Lanzarote, rear admiral's capsized on a wretched reef, claiming a hundred and one (8)
16 Central ring of what sounds like the pulse of a Massachusetts community (8)
17 Canadian island, super back in the 60s before the dénouement of French film (6)
18 Plant study in Australia to overlook the bay (6)
19 Part of Canada is derived from that French abbey in Normandy (6)
20 One place of discovery turned up to be an Indonesian island (4)

quick 1

Across

1 First god of the Hindu triad (6)
4 Spits which join islands to the mainland (8)
9 Continental section of Equatorial Guinea (3,4)
11 Scottish natural region centred on Dundee (7)
12 Greek goddess of victory (4)
13 Mediaeval Tuscan city (5)
14 Inland 31 (4)
17 Sea of the west Atlantic, the breeding ground of eels (8)
18 Pieces of Hindu music (5)
20 Legal capital of Bolivia, named after Simon Bolivar's second-in-command (5)
22 Collective designation of the League of Five Nations in N America, c 1570 (8)
26 One of the world's staple crops, particularly in Asia (4)
27 6 with the fastest-running tides in the world (5)
28 Province of Albania and its capital, near the site of ancient Apollonia (4)
30 British royal dynasty (7)
32 Descendants of the Phoenicians (7)
33 Island, one of a chain off S Florida (3,5)
34 6 in Australia named in 1770 after a study by Sir Joseph Banks (6)

Down

1 31 in the Arctic north of the European continent (7)
2 6 where Nelson defeated the French in the battle of the Nile in 1798 (7)
3 Hawaiian island (4)
5 Belgian ferry port (6)
6 Open-mouthed inlet of 31 (3)
7 German city whose St Thomas' church is associated with JS Bach (7)
8 In oceanography, the shallows immediately off continental shores (7)
10 Most frigid (6)
15 Swiss city on the Rhine, in the German spelling (5)
16 Middle-eastern national (5)
19 NE or SE winds blowing towards the equator (6)
20 Exclave of Malaysia on the island of Borneo (7)
21 One, traditionally, born within the sound of Bow bells (7)
23 Japanese island taken by the Americans in 1945 (7)
24 Atlantic island formed from a subterranean volcano in 1963 (7)
25 Saharan nomad (6)
29 Italian river, source in the Apennines (4)
31 The greater part of the earth's surface (3)

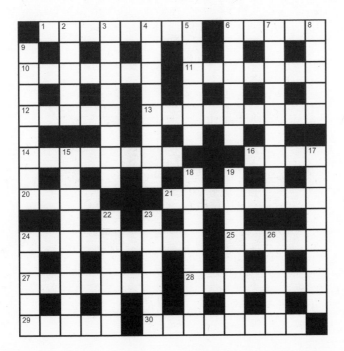

quick 2

Across

1 Region of N Greece, capital Larissa (8)
6 Iraqi oil port (5)
10 Industrial port of Jutland, Denmark (7)
11 University town of S England, immortalized by Oscar Wilde, who was imprisoned there (7)
12 City of Alabama known in the 1960s for its Civil Rights marches (5)
13 Canadians of the westernmost prairies (9)
14 Capital of Moldova (8)
16 Malaysian port, capital of Perak state (4)
20 Egyptian isthmus, a vital international sea link (4)
21 State capital of N Dakota, Custer's base before the Little Big Horn (8)
24 C American country bordered by Mexico, Belize, El Salvador and Honduras (9)
25 Ancient Euphrates city, home of the oldest recorded Hamito-Semitic language (5)
27 City of S India, the capital of mediaeval Pandiya (7)
28 Major seaport of SE Spain, as known in the Valencian dialect (7)
29 Poet assassinated in the Spanish Civil War and a market town in Murcia (5)
30 The main island of a country set off the coast of Venezuela (8)

Down

2 Meat slaughtered in accordance with Islamic law (5)
3 One of the 'new' European countries of the 1990s, capital Bratislava (8)
4 Oceanic inlet of S Africa in which sits Port Elizabeth (5,3)
5 Major ethnic and language group of Nigeria... (6)
6 ...its Ibo homeland which fleetingly grasped independence in the 1960s (6)
7 Pakistani city of the Sind; Indian dormitory town for Delhi (9)
8 Scots county effectively reborn in 1996 with the break up of Tayside Region (5)
9 Kneeling pads in church: W Sussex town (8)
15 Norseman settler from the 9th century, independent since 1944 (9)
17 Port of Hokkaido, Japan (8)
18 Port of Kyushu, Japan (8)
19 City of Maharashtra, the biggest cotton market in India (8)
22 Native American tribe giving name to a French trading post on the Illinois River (6)
23 Adherent of a 7th century Chinese philosophical system ascribed to Lao-tzu (6)
24 Russian name for the Belarus city of Homyel (5)
26 ----- Lumpur, the missing bit meaning estuary or river confluence (5)

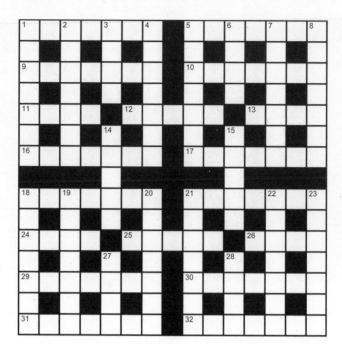

quick 3

Across

1 Sagarmatha, to the Nepalese (7)
5 French poetic form and a settlement in Mauritius (7)
9 European country, capital Bucharest (7)
10 Indian Ocean archipelago positioned between the Andaman Islands and Sumatra (7)
11 Quick marriage & divorce capital of the US? (4)
12 Islamic holy war (alternative spelling) (5)
13 See 19 Down
16 Hindu deities as manifested in human form (7)
17 Longest river in Ireland (7)
18 Citizen of an Arabic country (7)
21 Lakes area predominantly in the Swiss canton of Neuchatel (5)
24 Arabic royal family (4)
25 Department and oasis of Algeria (5)
26 US university since 1887; a college at the New Haven site since 1716 (4)
29 Portuguese Atlantic island (7)
30 Basque homeland (7)
31 Uninhabited Caribbean island, part of Antigua and Barbuda (7)
32 One of a federation of states in the Gulf (7)

Down

1 Area of Stoke-on-Trent named by Josiah Wedgwood after a pre-Roman area of Italy (7)
2 Egyptian industrial city on the Nile near Hermopolis and other ruins (2,5)
3 Lough and river of Ireland (4)
4 Saharan nomads (7)
5 Inhabitants of the Friendly Islands, capital Nuku'alofa (7)
6 Pre-Conquest civilization of S America (4)
7 Eastern Mediterranean country (7)
8 Modern industrial city in Coahuila state, Mexico (7)
14 Central Asian descended from Persian-speaking Iranians (5)
15 Capital of Oregon state (5)
18 Mountainous region of ongoing disputes between Pakistan and India (7)
19/13 Last major US Army/Sioux battle, tragically recalled in 1973 (7,4)
20 The Hoosier State, the nineteenth state of the Union (7)
21 Language of Thailand (7)
22 Largest desert in S America (7)
23 England-Wales border around Chester (7)
27 Scandinavian whose language is akin to Estonian (4)
28 Province, and its capital, of Lombardy, famed for sparkling wine (4)

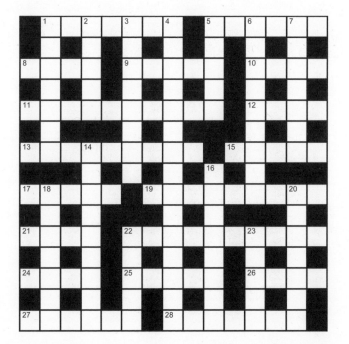

quick 4

Across

1 Capital of Wales (7)
5 Capital of Eritrea (6)
8 Sultanate, capital Muscat (4)
9 Island site of Vanuatu's capital, Vila (5)
10 Sea, part of the Antarctic Ocean (4)
11 Largest area of fresh water in the world (5,5)
12 Second city of the Republic of Ireland (4)
13 Highest peak (4550m) in Iran's Zagros Mts (6,3)
15 Burgundian city of gourmands, at the end of the Côte d'Or (5)
17 Capital of the French department of the Corrèze (5)
19 Largest town in the Outer Hebrides (9)
21 Capital of Samoa (4)
22 Industrial city of Bihar (10)
24 Almost always dry Saharan watercourse (4)
25 Capital of Cape Verde Is (5)
26 River, the world's eighth largest, forming much of the Russo-Chinese border (4)
27 Autonomous Chinese island in the S China Sea (6)
28 Industrial port of 22 (7)

Down

1 England county formed in 1974 from Westmorland, among others (7)
2 Andalusian hill town, popular with tourists, on the R Guadalevin gorge (5)
3 Town near the Ruhr, the largest in Sauerland (8)
4 Germany's financial centre (9-2-4)
5 Sandstone rock, now commonly called Uluru (5)
6 Centre of the Venezuelan oil industry (9)
7 Argentinian river port (7)
14 Describes the coast of former Yugoslavia (9)
16 Benevolent Hindu mother goddess (8)
18 Swedish university town (7)
20 Island near the Strait of Hormuz disputed by Iran and the Emirates (3,4)
22 Country off mainland Asia comprising of thousands of volcanic islands (5)
23 Capital of Bangladesh (5)

quick 5

Across

1 US state capital, named after a German leader (8)
5 African country, capital Kampala (6)
9 Address for a European married woman in colonial India (8)
10 1,000-year-old Romanian city, capital of Bihor county (6)
12 Island in the Firth of Clyde, so-called 'Scotland in miniature' (5)
13 Headland which marks the furthest point west in Asia (4,5)
14 Japan's fourth-largest city (6)
16 Mohammedan (7)
19 Caribbean island claimed by an Irishman in 1865 who created an 'aristocracy' based on literary figures (7)
21 Resort town of Queensland, Australia (6)
23 Town and airport of Grand-Terre Island, Guadeloupe (3,6)
25 Tuscan city famed for its Palio horse races (5)
26 Troubled West Bank city (6)
27 Inhabitant of a major city in S Belgium (8)
28 US state since 1959 (6)
29 Town of N France whose cathedral possesses the highest choir in the world (8)

Down

1 Former name of the Indian city of Mumbai (6)
2 Ancient Uzbek city, destroyed progressively by Alexander the Great and Genghis Khan (9)
3 Second city (variant spelling) of Abu Dhabi, on the Omani frontier (2,3)
4 Portuguese cathedral city with university origins going back to 1290 (7)
6 Italian Risorgimento hero (9)
7 Moroccan port with smuggling links to the nearby Spanish enclave of Melilla (5)
8 Mexico's premier Pacific resort (8)
11 Town on the inland road from Oman into Abu Dhabi (4)
15 Industrial city of Lower Saxony, Germany, birthplace of Erich Maria Remarque (9)
17 32nd State of the Union, capital St Paul (9)
18 Name of an Asian island nation before 1972 (3,5)
20 ---- River, battle in the Crimean War, 1854 (4)
21 Former Spanish kingdom covering much of the Iberian plateau (7)
22 St Paul's home town in Asia Minor (6)
24 Home-born Israeli (5)
25 Port on the R Niger, in Mali (5)

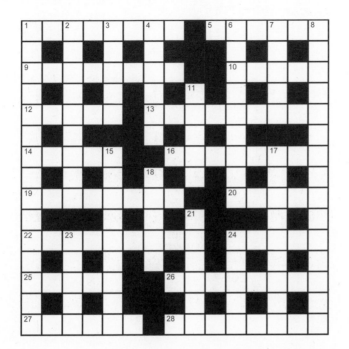

quick 6

Across
1 -------- Islands, of the W Mediterranean (8)
5 Indian of Persian descent (6)
9 Stronghold of Bernardo O'Higgins during the Chilean revolution (8)
10 Natives of Djibouti and troubled parts of Ethiopia and Eritrea (5)
12 Aboriginal name of Ayers Rock (5)
13 Relating to the island of Sri Lanka (9)
14 World's second highest mountain range (5)
16 Capital of the Mexican state of Baja California (8)
19 Capital of Virginia (8)
20 S African gold town named after the hero of a Sir Walter Scott novel (5)
22 Pertaining to ancient Brittany (9)
24 French resort on L Geneva, known for its water (5)
25 Name or part-name of several S African rivers, 'great' in Afrikaans (5)
26 Kent port and resort (8)
27 City and province of Turkey (6)
28 Ascetic adherents to a philosophy and religion akin to Buddhism (8)

Down
1 Disorienting area between Florida, Cuba and another place? (7,8)
2 Ancient part of the French Midi (6,3)
3 Tokelau's largest atoll (5)
4 Brazilian river famous for its 275 waterfalls (6)
6 One from Asia Minor (9)
7 River of NW USA, the Columbia's main tributary (5)
8 Citizens of Polynesian Rapa Nui (6,9)
11 County of W Wales dismantled in 1996 (5)
15 Citizen of West Bank town Sebastiyah during New Testament times (9)
17 Episcopalians (9)
18 Site of a holy shrine in Co Mayo, Ireland (5)
21 Capital of Turkey (6)
23 Native of Aotearoa (5)
24 Major German industrial city of the Ruhr (5)

quick 7

Across

1 Mining town near Reno, Nevada (6)
4 Honshu city near Osaka (7)
8 Town in SE Alabama from a biblical place named in Genesis (6)
9 Most populated Canadian province (7)
12 Town in Berkshire, England, home to the Meteorological Office (9)
13 Gaelic language (5)
14 Port of upper Normandy (2,5)
15 Port of N Luzon (7)
17 Ethnic group and language based around the Ganges-Brahmaputra delta (7)
19 Towns sharing the same name in California, Colombia and Venezuela (7)
21 The second Finnish city (5)
23 German wine city on the Neckar, north of Stuttgart (9)
24 Major city and prefecture of Kyushu (7)
25 Inhabitants of Nunavut (6)
26 Nomad of the Syrian desert (7)
27 Indic language of the gypsies (6)

Down

1 Former French Foreign Legion HQ in Algeria (4,3,5)
2 Caspian Sea port at the head of the Volta delta (9)
3 Second city, and former capital of, the Ukraine (7)
5 Eastern 17 folk (12)
6 County town of Berkshire, England (7)
7 City of Guizhou province, China, east of Guiyang (5)
10 Mining town of Botswana, created in 1966 (6-6)
11 Rulers of China, 1644-1912, aka Manchu (5,7)
16 Capital of Montenegro (9)
18 Galician spelling of the major seaport of NW Spain (1,6)
20 Capital of Huila province, Angola, formerly Serra da Bandeira (7)
22 Department of Peru, and its capital dating back to 1588 (5)

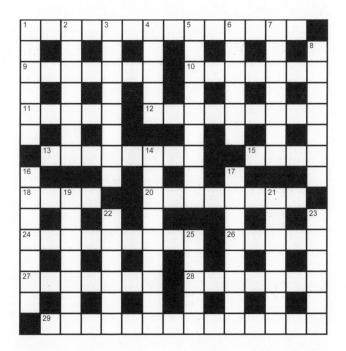

quick 8

Across

1/18/2 Across Great Britain (4,5,3,2,4,1,6)
9 Region of N Spain famed for its red wine (2,5)
10 Pre-Roman region of central Italy (7)
11 Fourth city of the Congo Republic, a sugar-producing town (5)
12 -- --- ---- City, formerly Saigon (2,3,4)
13 Capital of Paraguay (8)
15 One of the two main branches of Islam (4)
18 See 1
20 Equatorial sea area infamous for its long calm spells (8)
24 Sumatran city, close to the heart of the 2004 tsunami disaster (5,4)
26 River rising in the Tien Shan range and a tributary, eventually, of the Syr Darya (5)
27 Native American language and tribe of New England, akin to 16 (7)
28 Ancient Spanish city, once the haunt of Castilian kings (7)
29 World's second-largest cruise ship departure port, in Florida (4,10)

Down

1 City of Sichuan province at the confluence of the Yangtze and the Wu (6)
2 See 1 Across
3 Asians who replaced monarchism with communism in 1975 (8)
4 S Wales town, home of actors Richard Burton and Ray Milland (5)
5 (International) waterway opened in 1869 (4,5)
6 Relating to a European tall, blond people (6)
7 Branch of the Ural-Altaic language group (7)
8 One of Islam's great cities, sacked by Mongols, Tamerlane, Persians – and Americans (7)
14 Former Vietnam, Laos and Cambodia (9)
16 Native Americans of the Algonquin language group (7)
17 Resort town, the summer capital of India's Jammu and Kashmir state (8)
19 Dutch manufacturing town of Overijssel province, on the German border (7)
21 Region of the Czech Republic, chief town Brno (7)
22 Coastal town in Hampshire, England (6)
23 Of Catholics in Eastern Orthodox Churches (6)
25 Pious, often mystical, Jew (5)

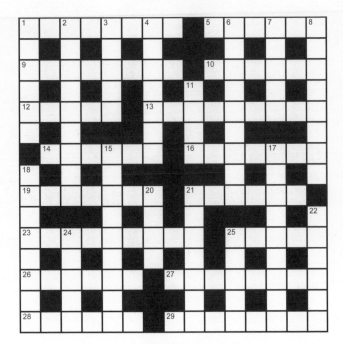

quick 9

Across

1 US state capital, named after a German leader (8)
5 African country, capital Kampala (6)
9 Address for a European married woman in colonial India (8)
10 1,000-year-old Romanian city, capital of Bihor county (6)
12 Island in the Firth of Clyde, so-called 'Scotland in miniature' (5)
13 Headland which marks the furthest point west in Asia (4,5)
14 Japan's fourth-largest city (6)
16 Mohammedan (7)
19 Caribbean island claimed by an Irishman in 1865 who created an 'aristocracy' based on literary figures (7)
21 Resort town of Queensland, Australia (6)
23 Town and airport of Grand-Terre Island, Guadeloupe (3,6)
25 Tuscan city famed for its Palio horse races (5)
26 Troubled West Bank city (6)
27 Inhabitant of a major city in S Belgium (8)
28 US state since 1959 (6)
29 Town of N France whose cathedral possesses the highest choir in the world (8)

Down

1 Former name of the Indian city of Mumbai (6)
2 Ancient Uzbek city, destroyed progressively by Alexander the Great and Genghis Khan (9)
3 Second city (variant spelling) of Abu Dhabi, on the Omani frontier (2,3)
4 Portuguese cathedral city with university origins going back to 1290 (7)
6 Italian Risorgimento hero (9)
7 Moroccan port with smuggling links to the nearby Spanish enclave of Melilla (5)
8 Mexico's premier Pacific resort (8)
11 Town on the inland road from Oman into Abu Dhabi (4)
15 Industrial city of Lower Saxony, Germany, birthplace of Erich Maria Remarque (9)
17 32nd State of the Union, capital St Paul (9)
18 Name of an Asian island nation before 1972 (3,5)
20 ---- River, battle in the Crimean War, 1854 (4)
21 Former Spanish kingdom covering much of the Iberian plateau (7)
22 St Paul's home town in Asia Minor (6)
24 Home-born Israeli (5)
25 Port on the R Niger, in Mali (5)

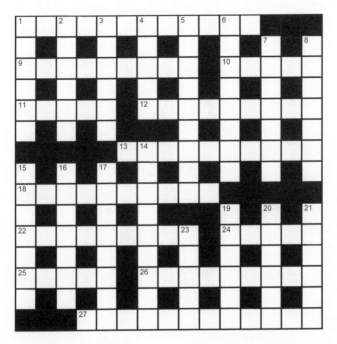

quick 10

Across

1 Previous name for Botswana (12)
9 New --------, a province of Canada (9)
10 Historic capital of Flanders (5)
11 Chicago's international airport (5)
12 Region of the world which takes its name from the Greek, meaning 'opposite the Great Bear' (9)
13 Form of cultural nationalism in the Middle East (3-7)
18 Costa Rican banana port (10)
22 Soviet name for Qaraghandy, Kazakhstan (9)
24 One of the main islands of Vanuatu (5)
25 Welsh industrial town with a 12C abbey and Norman castle (5)
26 Port, a former penal colony, of Australia (9)
27 Body of water separating Nunavut from Quebec (6,6)

Down

1 Phoenician city said to give its name to the Bible as local papyrus was used in book production (6)
2 Eponymous head of the Il Khanate, one of the four major divisions in the Mongol Empire (6)
3 One of Ireland's four ancient provinces (6)
4 Currency of Nigeria (5)
5 Original name of a body of water in Ethiopia, the source of the Blue Nile (4,5)
6 Citizen of a W African country (8)
7 Of the triangular alluvia-filled areas near river mouths (7)
8/21 Arid strip in N Chile, S Peru (7,6)
14 Italy's spinal range of mountains (9)
15 City of Washington State, a major transportation centre on the Columbia R (7)
16 San ------- Fault, the interface of the E Pacific and N American tectonic plates (7)
17 Capital of Zhejiang province, China (8)
19 Eastern Mediterranean shore (6)
20 Suburb of Helsinki, granted separate city status in 1972 (6)
21 See 8
23 Nile dam (5)

quick 11

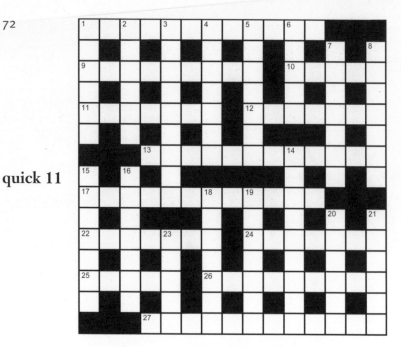

Across

1 The world's highest navigable waterway (4,8)
9 Middle European, recently independent (9)
10 Chinese city of Henan province, south of Zhengzhou (5)
11 Balearic Islanders (7)
12 Mountainous region of ongoing disputes between Pakistan and India (7)
13 The world's sixth-largest watercourse (5,7)
17 Inlet of the Atlantic at Rio de Janeiro (9,3)
22 Baltic island as the Danes call it (7)
24 Highest peak (4395 m) in the US Cascade Range (7)
25 Province, and its capital, of southern Turkey (5)
26 Spanish port from classical times (9)
27 Atlantic islanders, off the coast of Senegal (4,8)

Down

1 Burmese city, the largest in southern Shan state (6)
2 Province of central Finland and its capital (6)
3 Madagascan port (9)
4 Italian port and resort, historically part of Austria (7)
5 Capital of the Republic of Guinea (7)
6 Pre-Roman occupiers of Gaul, Britain and Ireland (5)
7 Old name for Taiwan; 'beautiful' in Portuguese (7)
8 South ------, the first British territory invaded by Argentina in the Falklands War (7)
14 Region of NW Botswana (9)
15 Warm ocean current off the SE African coast (7)
16 Enclave of Malaysia on the island of Borneo (7)
18 Department of France, capital Privas (7)
19 Scottish industrial town east of Glasgow (7)
20 Burundi city, formerly a royal residence (6)
21 Norfolk ------, recreational and ecologically important wetlands in E England (6)
23 Largest Basque province in Spain, capital Vitoria (5)

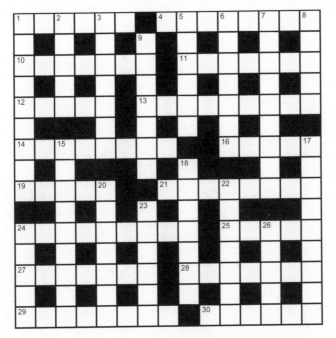

quick 12

Across

1 See 27
4 Flood control on L Nasser (5,3)
10 Relating to the arid region of N Africa (7)
11 Russian naval port on the Sea of Okhotsk (7)
12 City of Shandong province, south of Jinan (5)
13 Sacred mountain in Sri Lanka, Samanala in Sinhalese (5,4)
14 Strait linking the Atlantic to the Pacific (8)
16 Seaport of N Chile (5)
19 German name for the longest European river to empty into the Atlantic (5)
21 Malawian city named after the birthplace of David Livingstone (8)
24 Nomadic people of SW Africa (9)
25 Indigenous people of the W Hemisphere's Arctic (5)
27&1 Island chains which together formed a British colony between 1915 and 1975 (7 & 6)
28 18 in Africa, straddling the Nigeria-Cameroon border (7)
29 Cotton trousers from the old name for Nanjing (8)
30 Premier French ferry port (6)

Down

1 New, troubled Asian democracy, capital, Dili (4,5)
2 Finnish industrial town on L Paijanne (5)
3 Chilean site of a WWI naval battle in 1914 (7)
5 One of the Polynesian groups of people (6)
6 In Georgia, the home of golf's Masters Tournament (7)
7 'Cowboy capital' of the Old West, site of the Boot Hill graveyard (5,4)
8 Capital of Belarus (5)
9 Citizen of an Indian offshore dependency (7)
15 Scottish defile running NE-SW which includes Lochs Ness and Linnhe (5,4)
17 N Pacific archipelago (9)
18 State of Nigeria, capital Jos (7)
20 Zulu of Guateng and Matabeleland (7)
22 Industrial port of Honshu (7)
23 ------ Island, southernmost borough of New York City (6)
24 Germany city of the Rhine Westphalia on the Ennepe River (5)
26 Honshu city, capital of Saitama prefecture (5)

quick 13

Across

1 The Basque language (7)
5 ------- and Barbuda, Caribbean state (7)
9 Urals city and river (5)
10 Cities of India and Pakistan with more than 1m population, sharing the same name (9)
11 Place in Cambridgeshire, home to strong English cheese... (7)
12 ...and a Dutch city famous for its Edam market (7)
13 Relating to an Atlantic island touching the Arctic Circle (9)
16 Europe's highest active volcano (4)
18 ---- Strait, separating Victoria and Tasmania (4)
19 Channel separating Europe and Asia (9)
22 City of greater St Petersburg, founded on ironworks (7)
23 Capital of Libya (7)
25 Former name of the Anatolian region, approximating modern-day Turkey (4,5)
26 ----- al Arab, river formed from the confluence of the Tigris and Euphrates (5)
27 Siberian city on the Chulym R, a tributary of the Ob (7)
28 Peoples whose capital in the New Testament was Antioch (7)

Down

1 Andean volcano, NE of Arequipa, Peru (2,5)
2 Bantu people of southern central Africa (5)
3 Of a part of Europe, sometime German, now French (8)
4 Largest lake in the Tyrolean Alps (5)
5 See 23
6 Thrace, as in the Greek (6)
7 British dependency on mainland Europe (9)
8 Pyrenean principality (7)
14 Hampshire town whose airfield (now Southampton Airport) saw the first flight of the Spitfire fighter plane (9)
15 Resort on the Dalmatian coast, Ragusa of old to Italians (9)
17 Hindu religious city of Kerala state (8)
18 Historic Uzbek city, home to an important Tajik minority (7)
20 Town of the Charente-Maritime, France, and former provincial capital (7)
21 Special Chinese economic zone facing Taiwan (6)
23/5 British dependency in the Caribbean, capital Cockburn Town (5,3,6)
24 US Headquarters of the Strategic Air Command (5)

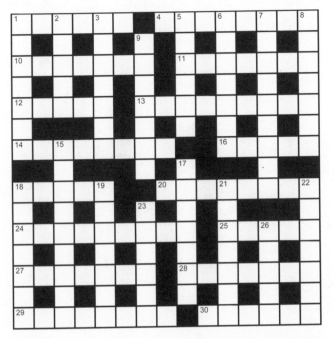

quick 14

Across

1 Egyptian industrial city, SE of Cairo (6)
4 Capital of the ancient Hindu Kakatiya Empire in Andhra Pradesh (8)
10 Former gold-mining town in Victoria, Australia, named after a local boxer (7)
11 City of Taiwan near the western shore road from Taipei to Tainan (7)
12 French alpine lake resort (5)
13 Sumatran city, capital of an Indonesian special territory (5,4)
14 Citizen of an African nation, part of which formed ancient Nubia (8)
16 Hokkaido coal-exporting port (5)
18 Indonesian province and its capital, aka Telanaipura (5)
20 Asian country created in 1947 (8)
24 German river port linked to the Rhine-Ruhr region by the Mittelland canal (9)
25 Swiss mountain (3970 m), its north face providing a constant challenge to climbers (5)
27 Modern day Hibernia (7)
28 Nigerian brewery city on the Niger R (7)
29 Scotland's 'Granite City' (8)
30 Capital of the ancient Anjou province in France (6)

Down

1 Book of the Old Testament and a letter in the New? (7)
2 Pineapple-producing Hawaiian island, west of Maui (5)
3 Home to the Popes between 1309-77 (7)
5 City of Henan province, the seat of the Yin (Shang) dynasty (6)
6 Uto-Aztecan American of the Great Plains (7)
7 Former, colonial, name of Ghana (4,5)
8 Capital of Gansu province, formerly Lanchow (7)
9 Major beach resort of E Africa (7)
15 Capital of the Negros Oriental province of the Philippines (9)
17 Asian kingdom's capital since 1782 (7)
18 Caribbean island, capital Kingston (7)
19 Nordic republic with full autonomy since 1944 (7)
21 Portuguese or Spanish (7)
22 Scandinavian raiders who settled in NW France (7)
23 Scotland's fourth city, on the R Tay (6)
26 Canadian peninsula, a northern extension of the Appalachians (5)

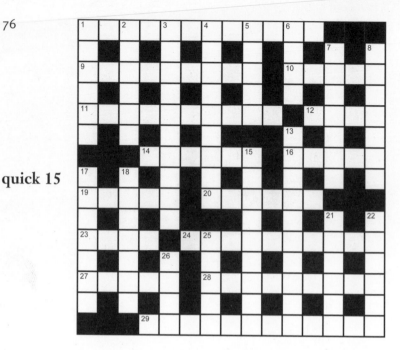

quick 15

Across

1 Port on the middle Rhine (12)
9 Capital of Mpumalanga province, S Africa (9)
10 17 country, capital Porto Novo (5)
11 Continent whose coastline was only explored as recently as 1820 (10)
12 River of Siberia (4400 km), the world's ninth longest (4)
14 See 25 Down
16 ---- culture, an ancient civilization of Ohio (5)
19 The modern Persian language (5)
20 Generically, along with the Mongol, one of the hordes of Genghis Khan (6)
23 Modern country based on ancient Mesopotamia (4)
24 17 capital, since 1879, built as a new city (5,5)
27 Seaport of N Chile (5)
28 French river valley and alpine resort (3,6)
29 Californian and Spanish mountain ranges sharing the same name (6,6)

Down

1 City of Zhejiang province, E China (6)
2 Minnesota town at the western extremity of L Superior (6)
3 Agricultural city in NE Brazil, south of Belem on the Tocantins R (10)
4 German manufacturing city on the R Neckar (9)
5 Native Mexican dominant between the 12th and 15th centuries (5)
6 European river forming part of the frontier between the old GDR and FDR (4)
7 European river flowing through Russia, Belarus and Ukraine (7)
8 Algerian oasis on the trans-Saharan route (2,5)
13 City in the Greater Recife conurbation of Brazil's Pernambuco state (10)
15 Costa Rican volcano (3339 m) in Cartago department (9)
17 One from the Dark Continent (7)
18 Ancient Greece associated with bucolic innocence (7)
21 Upmarket suburb of San Diego (2,4)
22 Illinois town named after its lead mines (6)
25/14 Narrowest part of the English Channel (5,6)
26 17 country, capital Bamako (4)

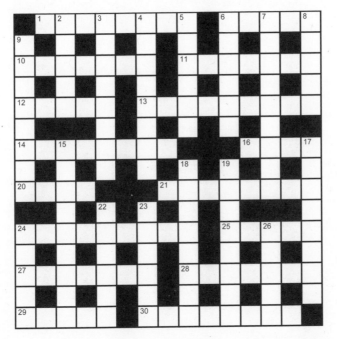

quick 16

Across
1 Province of NE Thailand and its capital (4,4)
6 Citizen of a Russian Federation republic, capital Kazan (5)
10 African country, capital Asmara (7)
11 Sea battle in which Themistocles defeated Xerxes in 480BC (7)
12 See 3 Down
13 Site of an Anglo-French battle in 1415 (9)
14 Site of a British-Dervish battle in 1898 (8)
16 Italian active volcano (4)
20 Norfolk town where the R Waveney forms the border with Suffolk (4)
21 Welsh castle town, the origins of the Tudor dynasty (8)
24 Madagascan thermal spa resort, south of Antananarivo (9)
25 Capital of Morocco (5)
27 ------- and Ellice Islands, former British Pacific colony (7)
28 Californian city's island setting on San Francisco Bay (7)
29 Russian region of Siberia, capital, Barnaul (5)
30 French river upon which the town of Cognac stands (8)

Down
2 The first autonomous Afro-American state in 1804 (5)
3/12 Inhabitants of a part of the UK (8,5)
4 Indigenous American, forced out of the Greater Antilles by Caribs (8)
5 Holy city of Rama and Sita on the Godavari R, NE of Mumbai (6)
6 Capital of Mexico state, in Mexico (6)
7 Anglicized spelling of a 12th century nomads' meeting place, now in Mali (9)
8 Capital of Gilan province, Iran (5)
9 Fois gras and truffle centre of France (8)
15 Desert of central Iran (5-1,3)
17 Pacific Islands, part of Alaska (8)
18 Area of Guyana famous for its cane sugar (8)
19 -------- Mountains, site of a Kenyan national park (8)
22 Industrial Honshu city, in the Kinki region, with a fine castle (6)
23 Sea, made up principally of the Gulfs of Bothnia and Finland (6)
24 Bay in S Africa where Port Elizabeth stands (5)
26 Breton naval base (5)

quick 17

Across

9 Ohio port on L Erie (9)
10 Capital of the French department, Pas-de-Calais (5)
11 Southern (7)
12 Egyptian industrial city on the Nile near Hermopolis and other ruins (2,5)
13 Native American tribe, from the Ohio valley, finally to be found on an Oklahoman reservation (5)
14 County town of Kent, England (9)
16 Polynesian Rapa Nui's inhabitants (6,9)
20 Citizens of a W African country (9)
23 Last Chinese dynasty, set up by the Manchus in 1644 (5)
24 Argentinean river port (7)
25 Figurehead of Roman power during New Testament times (7)
26 Industrial city facing Kolkata across the Hooghly (5)
27 Objects, traditions associated with this country (9)

Down

1 S American national (10)
2 Ancient peoples of the Middle East (8)
3 ------ Town, formerly the main port of Malaysia (6)
4 Spanish ------, Puerto Rican area of N Manhattan (6)
5 Site in Warwickshire of the first English Civil War battle, 1642 (8)
6 Of an Italian city renowned for its ham and cheese (8)
7 Province of N Italy and its capital (6)
8 Tasmania's highest mountain (1617 m) (4)
15 Citizen of the former GDR (4,6)
17 Of a pre-Roman culture in central Italy (8)
18 Brazilian dormitory town in the Rio de Janeiro conurbation (8)
19 E African independent national since 1993 (8)
21 Describing part of Aquitaine (6)
22 Part of the Union of Kalmar, 1397-1523, federation of European states (6)
23 Early Christian church with adherents still today in Egypt and other countries (6)
24 Tributary of the Rhine, the traditional industrial heart of Germany (4)

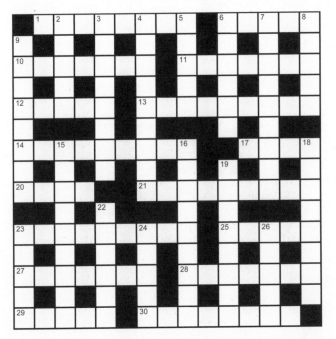

quick 18

Across

1 Kent port and resort (8)
6 Turkish province and its capital (5)
10 Belgian port (7)
11 Nomad of the Syrian desert (7)
12 Airport, harbour and fjord of SW Greenland (5)
13 Wine town north of San Francisco (5,4)
14 Southern extent of the tropics, as depicted on a map (9)
17 One of the Inner Hebrides (4)
20 Lough and river of N Ireland (4)
21 Tourist resort of Co Kerry, Ireland (9)
23 Peak looking down on Scotland's largest freshwater loch (3,6)
25 Colorado ski resort (5)
27 Second city of Fiji (7)
28 Col in the Himalayas well known to Everest climbers (3,4)
29 Largest city in Florida (5)
30 Panhandle city of Texas (8)

Down

2 Las Rias -----, wild coastline area of NW Spain
3 Ancient language of the Hindus (8)
4 Uluru (5,4)
5 Largest city in the Ruhr valley (5)
6 Native of a Middle-Eastern Arabic republic (6)
7 Citizen of British Columbia's provincial capital (9)
8 Capital of Yemen (5)
9 Native American of the SW of US and their Uto-Aztecan language (8)
15 Geomorphological term for a piece of land like the Peloponnese (9)
16 Estuarine distributaries of the world's longest river (4,5)
18 One from 'down in Demerara'? (8)
19 Arid plateau covering much of SW Africa (8)
22 Capital of the Comoros Islands (6)
23 Brazilian city, capital of Para state, at the mouth of the Tocantins R (5)
24 Japan's third city (5)
26 Wine town of the Cape; the Victor Verster prison is close by (5)

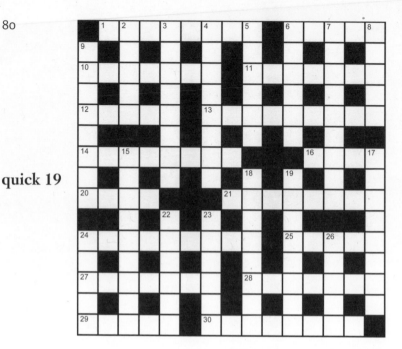

quick 19

Across

1 World's second highest active volcano (4169 m), on Hawaii (5,3)
6 Scottish administrative region, head town Forfar (5)
10 Siberian 'new town' on the Trans-Siberian Railway, constructed in 1949 (7)
11 Basque homeland (7)
12 French department, capital Grenoble (5)
13 Headlands sharing the same name in Antarctica and Vancouver I (4,5)
14 Follower of the architect of the Reformation (8)
16 Indian city, home to the Taj Mahal (4)
20 One of the Italian Lakes (4)
21 Port of Georgia, USA (8)
24 Capital of S Sumatra province, Indonesia (9)
25 Burgundy wine town, on the R Saone (5)
27 Historic Andalucian city where the Alhambra is to be found (7)
28 Alternative name to a Russian Federation Republic, capital Kazan (7)
29 Cornish cathedral city (5)
30 Port of Sabah, Malaysia (8)

Down

2 German people from whose name English was derived (5)
3 Vikings (8)
4 Body of water in N Central Africa (4,4)
5 Second city of Syria (6)
6 Umbrian town, the home of a 12-13th century saint (6)
7 Former Welsh county, headquarters Cardiff (9)
8 Turkish province and its capital (5)
9 French town which eventually, via its US namesake, gave its name to a motorcar (8)
15 State of S India (5,4)
17 Greek of ancient Attica (8)
18 Devon resort, part of the English 'Riviera' (8)
19 East coastal area of the Adriatic Sea (8)
22 Ecuadorean garden city of the Andes (6)
23 Amazon port near the confluence with the R Negro, 1000 miles from the open sea (6)
24 ----- Sound, natural inlet upon which sits Seattle (5)
26 Ancient area of Asia Minor, south of the Maeander R (5)

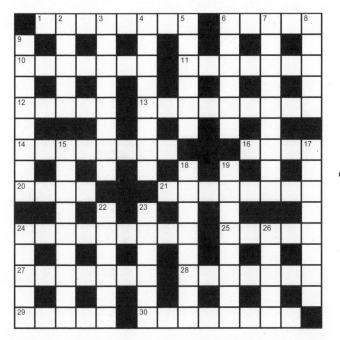

quick 20

Across

1 Capital of Alberta, Canada (8)
6 Capital of Bihar state, India (5)
10 Albanian province and its capital (7)
11 Windward I, subject to invasion by the US and others in 1983 (7)
12 Industrial Italian city, headquarters of the Italian Army during WW1 (5)
13/15 Dangerous rock and whirlpool in the Strait of Messina (6,3,9)
14 Of a mountainous Peloponnese district; synonymously describing a rustic paradise (8)
16 English (phonetic) spelling of Serbian city, birthplace of Constantine the Great (4)
20 Ancient Asian kingdom renamed in 1939 (4)
21 People of E Pyrenean Spain and France (8)
24 Ijssel Meer was formed in 1932 by damming this (6,3)
25 Pastoral people of Kenya and Tanzania (5)
27 Wisconsin's capital, named after the fourth President of the USA (7)
28 Towns in Berkshire and Pennsylvania sharing the same name (7)
29 Ancient city of Tigré, Ethiopia, with legendary connections to the Ark of the Covenant (5)
30 Ukrainian industrial city of the Donbas (8)

Down

2 One of the UAE and its capital (5)
3 European port, as spelt in Flemish (8)
4 Carthaginian, perhaps in a previous life (8)
5 Major Japanese city, capital of Aichi prefecture in Chubu region (6)
6 Prehistoric communal Native American culture (6)
7 Madagascan port, formerly Tamatave (9)
8 Islands in the Gulf of Bothnia belonging to Finland (5)
9 Capital of the French department of Oise (8)
15 See 13 Across
17 Former base of the Royal Fleet and a Cinq Port on the English south coast (8)
18 Pertaining to a group of islands off the Spanish mainland (8)
19 Californian city on the western edge of the Mohave Desert (8)
22 Norfolk river flowing through Norwich (6)
23 Sub-Saharan Africa: term used by anti-apartheid factions for S Africa itself (6)
24 City of S Malawi (5)
26 Middle European, one of whose four official languages is Romansch (5)

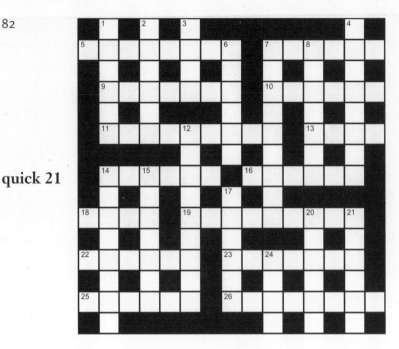

quick 21

Across

5 Major US river (2333 km) which joins the Mississippi south of Memphis (8)
7 Metropolitan ------ is divided into 96 departments (6)
9 Moldovan town, the ancient 'Gateway to Bessarabia' (7)
10 Turkish province and its capital (6)
11 Juarez's capital, 1862-67, of the (same-named) largest state in Mexico (9)
13 River rising in France and flowing north to join the German Mosel (4)
14 Brandy town of the Charente (6)
16 Capital of Canada (6)
18 Arizona city named after the monolithic flat-topped peaks of the locality (4)
19 Catalonian capital (9)
22 Country whose invasion in 1991 sparked off Operation Desert Storm (6)
23 N Ireland city, formerly 21's county town (7)
25 Seaport of New Zealand/Aotearoa, rebuilt after earthquake damage in 1932 (6)
26 Autonomous nation, part of the former Yugoslavia (8)

Down

1 Northern polar region (6)
2 Capital of the Central African Republic (6)
3 Piemonte wine city, SE of Turin (4)
4 Industrial city of Honshu, NE of Tokyo (8)
6 Commercial city on the Yangtze, west of Wuhan (6)
7 W Australia's largest port (9)
8 Shrinking Asian lake, once the world's fourth largest (4,3)
12 Capital of Mongolia (4,5)
14 Capital of Quintana Roo state, Mexico (8)
15 S American indigenous people of Paraguay and W Brazil (7)
17 World's southernmost active Volcano (6)
20 Desert area of Ethiopia disputed by Somalia (6)
21 One of the traditional six counties of Ulster, within N Ireland (6)
24 Third city of France, its gastronomic heart (4)

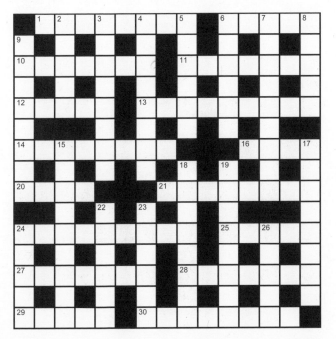

quick 22

Across

1 Region of SE Europe (8)
6 Indian Ocean islands, administered by Australia (5)
10 Province of SW Turkey, and its capital (7)
11 Predominantly Serbian region of Croatia, retaken from the Serbs in 1995 (7)
12 Capital of the Republic of Belau in the Caroline Is (5)
13 Dutch-derived language (9)
14 Of a mountainous Peloponnese district synonymous with a rustic paradise (8)
16 Alternative abbreviated form for the Dutch city of Dordrecht (4)
20 City of Madhya Pradesh, joined to the steel town of Bhilainagar (4)
21 Port of Georgia, USA (8)
24 Irian Jaya's seaport capital (9)
25 Trail in C Breton I named after the British explorer who landed there in 1497 (5)
27 Portuguese cathedral city with university origins going back to 1290 (7)
28 US city, host to the 1996 summer Olympic Games (7)
29 Administrative territory of N Brazil, capital Macapa (5)
30 Buckinghamshire town, the northernmost terminus in London's Underground railway (8)

Down

2 Largest alpine lake in Austria (5)
3 US rivers of the same name, emptying into the Gulfs of California and Mexico, respectively (8)
4 Sea area surrounded by islands in the Orkneys, also called ----- Flow (5,3)
5 Capital of Turkey (6)
6 Michigan home to the Hazeltine National GC, site of US Open and PGA Championships (6)
7 Citizen of the third city of the USA (9)
8 E Europeans whose principal alphabets are Latin and Cyrillic (5)
9 S Atlantic islands, aka Las Malvinas (8)
15 City of Espiritu Santu state, Brazil (9)
17 French Pacific islander (8)
18 Capital of Maramures county, Romania (4,4)
19 Portuguese town, the cockerel named after which is the national symbol (8)
22 African country, capital Lusaka (6)
23 S American country, capital Georgetown (6)
24 Asian capital's former spelling (5)
26 Islands in the Indonesian Moluccas (5)

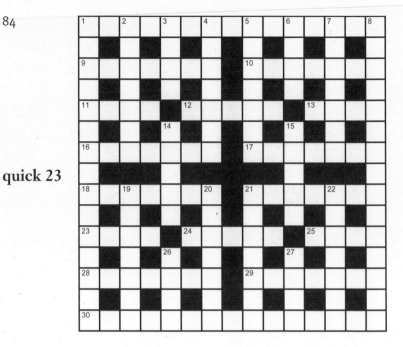

quick 23

Across

1 Forcible evacuation or extermination of a minority people from one area (6,9)
9 Former Dutch Guiana, capital Paramaribo (7)
10 N London suburb known for its film and TV studios (7)
11 River of western Germany (4)
12 Centre of Roman power in N Europe (5)
13 Latvian (4)
16 District of Uva province, Sri Lanka (7)
17 Venetian beach area (3,4)
18 City on the Volga for a while named Andropov (7)
21 C African (7)
23 ---- Depression, or Triangle, in Ethiopia and Djibouti (4)
24 Slav, for instance (5)
25 Part of the former French Indo China (4)
28 River and province of NE Turkey (7)
29 Department of Greek Macedonia and its capital (7)
30 Canadian island in the St Lawrence River (9,6)

Down

1 Part of the Arctic Ocean (4,8,3)
2 Oldest US university, founded in 1636 at Cambridge, Mass (7)
3 Scottish island where St Columba landed in 563 AD (4)
4 England county formed in 1974 from Westmorland, among others (7)
5 Sagarmatha, to those from 15 (7)
6 Scottish loch linked to the sea by the Caledonian Canal (4)
7 Citizen of the country 'born' in 1948 (7)
8 Tourist resort of Nicaragua known for its diving (5,4,6)
14 Alternative name for a Malaysian rubber port formerly called Port Sweetenham (5)
15 Asian country, capital Kathmandu (5)
19 Irish islands at the furthest point west in Europe (7)
20 Citizens of NE Asia (7)
21 Xinjiang city in the foothills of the Tien Shan Range (7)
22 Rio waterfront (7)
26 Largest of the 24 Dalmatian islands (4)
27 The ----, reclaimed marshland, primarily in the English counties of Cambridgeshire and Lincolnshire (4)

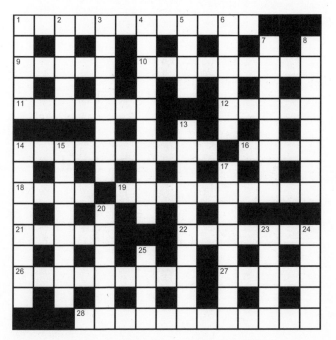

quick 24

Across

1 Bishop-governed Church; broader Anglican (12)
9 Russian lake in the Karelia republic (5)
10 Californian port and resort which became the permanent home of the Queen Mary in 1967 (4,5)
11 Brazilian state, capital Macaeio (7)
12 City in Honshu, west of Gifu (5)
14 North Atlantic Drift (4,6)
16 Mountain of Thessaly (1978m) featured in Greek myth (4)
18 Capital of the French department of Gers and of ancient Armagnac (4)
19 Ukrainian city as named between 1939 and 1992, originally Elizavetgrad (10)
21 Tamil Nadu cotton city on the R Cauvery (5)
22 Stone found in 1799 near Alexandria, a source for deciphering Egyptian hieroglyphics (7)
26 Citizens of the Yellowhammer State (9)
27 German industrial city in N Rhine-Westphalia (5)
28 Africans from the former French equatorial colonies (12)

Down

1 Classical Portuguese city, the Roman Liberalitas Julia (5)
2 Japanese city in the motor industry, NW of Osaka (5)
3 Region of the Landes department, SW France, noted for its foie gras (8)
4 Body of water separating India and Sri Lanka (4,6)
5 Capital of Upper Austria (4)
6 Old (poetic) name for Britain (6)
7 Former name of Ujung Pandang, Indonesia (8)
8 Asian country, capital Bangkok (8)
13 High plateau region of Brazil (4,6)
14 Cape Breton I town, once an important coal-mining centre (5,3)
15 French Mediterranean naval shipyards between Marseille and Toulon (2,6)
17 Capital of the Faero Is (8)
20 Malaysian state and its capital (6)
23 Second city of Oklahoma, a port on the Arkansas R (5)
24 Ancient region of France, around La Rochelle (5)
25 Capital of the Maldives (4)

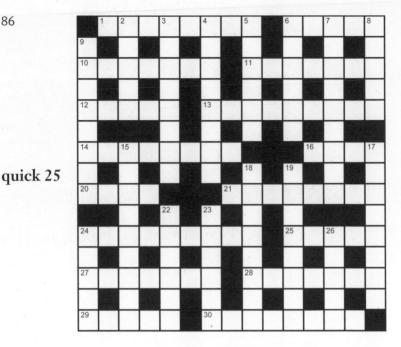

quick 25

Across

1 Region of Italy, roughly the 'toe' (8)
6 Algerian city established as French military post in 1748 (5)
10 Uto-Aztecan American of the Great Plains (7)
11 Antrim town based on flax after the arrival of Huguenots in 1694 (7)
12 Famous mission fort in San Antonio, Texas (5)
13 Site of the pivotal battle in the Western Desert, 1942 (2,7)
14 Black Sea territory of Georgia, classical Colchis (8)
16 Alternative name for the River Thames for part of its course (4)
20 14th century Mongol capital in Xinjiang province, formerly Wensu (4)
21 Serbian market town near Zica, where mediaeval kings were crowned (8)
24 Denizens of England's Lake District (9)
25 Constitutional capital of Bolivia; former unit of currency in Ecuador (5)
27 Home to the University of Wyoming (7)
28 Honshu city near Osaka (7)
29 Regional capital of the Drenthe province of the Netherlands (5)
30 Alabaman 'company town' between Birmingham and Atlanta (8)

Down

2 Warm wind of the French Massif Central (5)
3 Regions of Brazil, Colombia, Peru and Venezuela, all of the same name (8)
4 Colonial name for Zimbabwe (8)
5 ------ Alps that separate the Alps of Bavaria from Tyrol (6)
6 W African capital (6)
7 Swiss lake, as the Germans say (9)
8 Biblical river now the Jordanian Wadi Mujib (5)
9 Japanese resort renowned for its porcelain (8)
15 Inhabitants of a divided Himalayan region (9)
17 European country, capital Ljubljana (8)
18 European monarchy abolished in 1919 (8)
19 Citizens of the US' 49th state (8)
22 German industrial port on the R Weser (6)
23 Illinois town named after its lead mines (6)
24 World's deepest canyon, in the Peruvian Andes (5)
26 Province of N Argentina, capital Resistencia (5)

quick 26

Across

5 City of Venezuela, on the Orinoco (6,7)
8 ------ National Park in Alaska, named after the Aleut for Mt McKinley (6)
9 Seat of the Marquis of Bath, one of the first stately home safari parks (8)
10 One of the two main branches of Islam (4)
11 Of a city in ancient Illyria, near Fier in Albania (10)
12 Capital of the Vosges department in France, on the Moselle (6)
14 Corsica's second city (6)
17 Capital of the Toledo district of Belize with ferry links to Guatemala (5,5)
20 Ancient Greek site in Italy, an eponym for a school of philosophers including Zeno (4)
21 Battle in Bavaria in 1704 won by an ancestor of Winston Churchill (8)
22 French white wine town of the Bordeaux region (6)
23 French town on the Vienne, north of Futuroscope (13)

Down

1 Largest city of Assam (8)
2 City and (man-made) lake in Zimbabwe (6)
3 Hawaiian volcano, the world's second-tallest mountain from sea bed to peak (5,3)
4 Welsh castle town, its 19th century lord gave his name to garments with distinctive sleeve cuts (6)
5 The larger beneficiary of the 'Velvet Divorce' in 1993 (5,8)
6 Mountain in the Bible where King Saul defeated the Philistines (6)
7 Arid strip in N Chile, S Peru (7,6)
13 Welsh island, the Roman Mona, home of early British druidism (8)
15 Seat of the Dutch government (3,5)
16 Austrian alpine resort noted for its spectacular falls over three cascades (6)
18 One from the former Friendly Islands (6)
19 Breed of rabbit or cat, the former name for the Turkish capital (6)

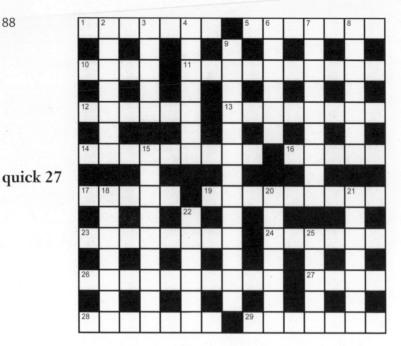

quick 27

Across

1 US river emptying into Chesapeake Bay (7)
5 Dagestan city, on the Caspian Sea (7)
10 Colombian city linked with drugs cartels (4)
11 Hebridean home in the end for George Orwell (4,2,4)
12 Resort city on the Costa del Sol (6)
13 One from Nassau, perhaps (8)
14 Supposed site of the final victory of Arthur's Britons over the invading Saxons (5,4)
16 S Korea's biggest port (5)
17 Russian small change (5)
19 Euskadi, in Spanish (4,5)
23 German city on the confluence of the Rhine and Neckar rivers (8)
24 Old name for Nova Scotia, before the ejection of the French (6)
26 She's a citizen of arguably the world's most chic capital (10)
27 Ethiopian formal language, still used in some Coptic services (4)
28 French river and department, capital Laval (7)
29 Capital of Italy's Veneto region (7)

Down

2 City SW of Tokyo, the gateway to the Izu Peninsula (7)
3 Official language of India's Orissa state (5)
4 Uttar Pradesh city where the Muslim University was set up as the Anglo-Oriental College in 1875 (7)
6 Saltwater pan (undrained river system) of Namibia (6)
7 Capital of Burundi (9)
8 Indian river, sacred to Hindus, flowing into the Gulf of Khambat (Cambay) (7)
9 Corollary of the so-called 'Greenhouse Effect' (6,7)
15 Californian seaside resort near San Diego (9)
18 Major railway junction of Honshu in Japan (7)
20 Language of Thailand (7)
21 Pertaining to a Ukrainian peninsula (7)
22 Mountain in Thessaly, appearing in Greek myth (6)
25 World's highest waterfall in a single uninterrupted cascade, in Venezuela (5)

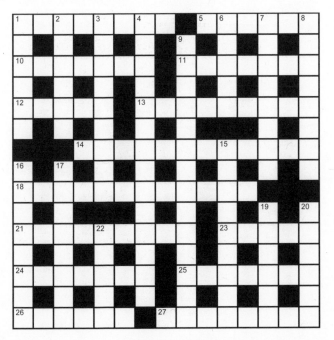

quick 28

Across

1 City of Uttar Pradesh, close to the Nepalese border (8)
5 Alternative name for Chippewa (6)
10 Destructive feature when earthquakes, etc, occur at sea (7)
11 Moravian city now part of the Czech Republic (7)
12 Semitic peoples of SW Asia and N Africa (5)
13 Citizen of a Commonwealth country, an Islamic republic (9)
14 Peak in central Greece, the home, myth has it, of he Muses (5,7)
18 Capital of Madagascar (12)
21 Second city of the Soviet Union (9)
23 German city, birthplace of Karl Marx (5)
24 Sri Lankan port and resort (7)
25 City of Henan, capital in the 12th century of the Chou dynasty (7)
26 One example of 12 (6)
27 Capital of Paraguay (8)

Down

1 City in E Turkey in the upper Tigris valley (6)
2 W African peoples centred on N Nigeria (6)
3 The only settlement on Pitcairn Is (9)
4 Cotswolds market town, a mediaeval wool centre (8,6)
6 Danish invaders of S and E England in the 5th century (5)
7 N Portuguese city, the original seat of the last royal family (8)
8 Name taken by some anti-apartheid supporters in S Africa: classically those from sub-Saharan Africa (8)
9 N England National Park cut by tributaries of the Ouse, eg, Aire and Wharfe (9,5)
15 Town on Long Island created for WWII veterans in 1947 (9)
16 Originally applied to barren country in S Dakota, now broadly used elsewhere (8)
17 N Indian city, capital of Arunachal Pradesh (8)
19 Of a N Indian state, capital Patna (6)
20 33rd State of the Union (1859), capital Salem (6)
22 Classical site in the Argolis valley of games held every 2nd and 4th year of an Olympiad (5)

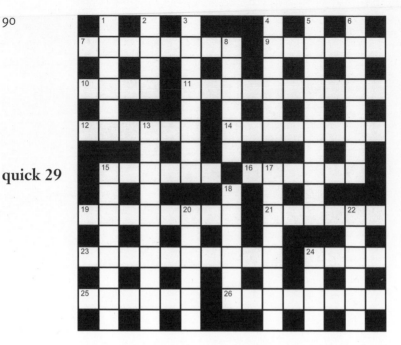

quick 29

Across

7 Largest leisure area in central London (4,4)
9 City of Benin, once the royal Dahomian capital (6)
10 Troubled city of Palestine (4)
11 One from a part of the Black Sea, also known as Adyghe or Adygey (10)
12 Imaginary line around the Earth indicating the end of the overhead sun's travel northwards (6)
14 -------- Alps or Sea, features around the Italian Riviera (8)
15 Pico ------, tallest mountain of the Dominican Rep and the W Indies (6)
16 Capital of Brittany (6)
19 Town, west of Detroit, home to the University of Michigan (3,5)
21 Guangdong city, formerly Namhoi, in the Pearl Delta, near Guangzhou (6)
23 The world's largest atoll, the Pacific Christmas I (10)
24 Cushtic language and people of N Ethiopia (4)
25 Honshu city on the Izu peninsula, in the shadow of Mt Fuji (6)
26 French department, capital Colmar (4-4)

Down

1 Native American people of the area around L Titicaca, straddling the Peru-Bolivia border (6)
2 German city noted for the Zeiss optical instrument company (4)
3 French town in the Vosges renowned for its crystal and a card game (8)
4 Upland Java resort south of Surubaya (6)
5 Arkansan National Park and the nearby town (3,7)
6 Hotel area of Paris, approximating the 4ème arondissement (2,6)
8 State of S India, capital Trivandrum (Thiruvananthapuram) (6)
13 Islands off the Moroccan coast, Spanish since 1847 (10)
15 Tamil Nadu city noted for its cheroots (8)
17 Egyptian industrial city, Egypt's biggest oasis (2,6)
18 One of N Ireland's traditional six counties, and its county town (6)
20 Capital of the Lebanon (6)
22 Moroccan resort, rebuilt after an earthquake in 1960 (6)
24 Turkish province on the Iranian border, and its capital (4)

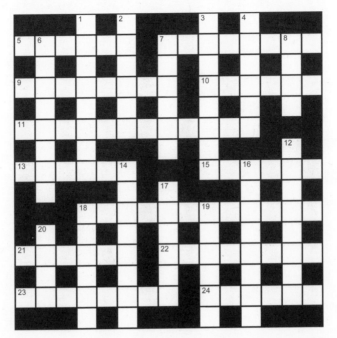

quick 30

Across

5 Himalayan peak (8150m), the world's 9th tallest (3,3)
7 Saskatchewan prairie town of the old Canadian Pacific Railroad (5,3)
9 Indian Ocean islands (8)
10 St Paul's home town in Asia Minor (6)
11 Scottish islet and lighthouse, the northernmost part of the UK (6,6)
13 Maharashtra city, near Mumbai (6)
15 Alabaman Gulf port (6)
18 S Hemisphere super-continent which began to break up in late Palaeozoic times (12)
21 Minnesota town at the western extremity of L Superior (6)
22 Capital of India finished in 1929 to a design by Sir Edward Lutyens (3,5)
23 Group of islands within the Seychelles archipelago (8)
24 French department, capital Moulins (6)

Down

1 Turkish village built on the former site of Hattusas, Hittite capital of old (8)
2 Fourth city of Zimbabwe (6)
3 Brazilian city, effectively a western suburb of Belo Horizonte (8)
4 District of C Portugal and its capital, dominated by a 12th century castle (6)
6 C American country, capital Tegucigalpa (8)
7 Mt ------, (2925m) in the Rhodope Range, Bulgaria's tallest peak (6)
8 River, the world's eighth largest, forming much of the Russo-Chinese border (4)
12 Scots skiing valley in the Grampians, near Braemar (4,4)
14 Sichuan city, E of Chengdu, on the Jialin R (8)
16 Holiday island off S Brittany (5-3)
17 Town in Matabeleland, developed on a large coalfield (6)
18 Armenian city, Leninakan between 1924-1991 (6)
19 London borough created in 1965 mainly from the old East and West Ham boroughs (6)
20 Scene of a US Pacific victory in 1942 (4)

quick 31

Across

7 Industrial city on the Volga, Kuibishev between 1935 and 1991 (6)
8 Island group in the NW Pacific (8)
9 Asians who replaced monarchism with communism in 1975 (8)
10 ------ Land, Antarctica, but outside the Antarctic Circle (6)
11 World's tallest mountain from seabed to peak (5,3)
12 Abbreviated form of the Russian region N Ossetia/------ (6)
13 International waterway opened in 1914 (6,5)
18 Brazilian river and city, capital of Mato Grosso state (6)
20 Hungary's third city (8)
22 Europe's largest lake (6)
23 Dem Rep of Congo port on the eponymous river, 1000 km inland (8)
24 Southernmost point of S America (4,4)
25 Californian citrus fruit centre to the east of Los Angeles (6)

Down

1 India's west coast named after an ancient Dravidian people (7)
2 Industrial town of the N Carolina piedmont (8)
3 Ex-county town of Scotland, on the R Clyde SE of Glasgow (6)
4 Brazilian river whose distributaries create the river island of Bananal (8)
5 Kiribati island, capital of the former Gilbert & Ellice Is (6)
6 Syrian port, facing Cyprus (7)
8 Arabian sultanate as known until 1970 (6,3,4)
14 Native Americans originally of the Great Plains and S Dakota (8)
15 Welsh town or Kenyan mountains (8)
16 State of NW India created in 1960 (7)
17 Uttar Pradesh lake, a holy place for Sikhs (7)
19 ------ High, subtropical N Atlantic anticyclone (6)
21 Wheat-growing area around Chartres, familiarly the 'breadbasket of France' (6)

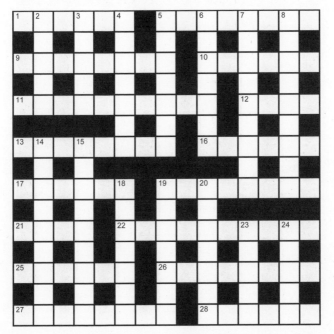

quick 32

Across

1 Capital of New Caledonia (6)
5 Aegean islands (8)
9 City of the Rhine, home to a school of German classical music in the 18th century (8)
10 Hungarian town, the site of a battle in 1526 which resulted in an Ottoman victory (6)
11 Site of the Treaty of European Union, 1992 (10)
12 Second Czech city, in Moravia (4)
13 Mid-Westerner, for example (8)
16 Heartland of the former Soviet Union (6)
17 Area of ancient and modern Greece near 28 (6)
19 Scene of a huge volcanic explosion in 1883 (8)
21 Ancient capital of northern Spain (4)
22 Formerly Southern Rhodesian (10)
25 Australia's northernmost community, on Cape York Peninsula (6)
26 Asian river which trends west from the Pamirs to empty into the Aral Sea (3,5)
27 Part of the Pacific in Indonesia (alternative spelling) (5,3)
28 Host city of the first modern Olympics, 1896 (6)

Down

2 Textile city of Punjab province, Pakistan (5)
3 Main tribal group of Rajasthan (5)
4 French department, capital, Rodez (7)
5 Loose economic association of Warsaw Pact countries (7)
6 Grey Cairns of -------, prehistoric site in Caithness, Scotland (7)
7 River and lake of west central Canada (9)
8 Californian city near the Palomar Observatory, in a citrus fruit area (9)
14 Paris' premier cathedral (5,4)
15 Papua Barat, as of February 2007 (5,4)
18 Georgian muslims living autonomously by the Black Sea (7)
19 Capital of Uganda (7)
20 ------- Sea, between the Timor Sea and the Torres Strait (7)
23 Cape -----, promontory of NW Scotland (5)
24 Strictly, a member of the peoples speaking any Indo-European language (5)

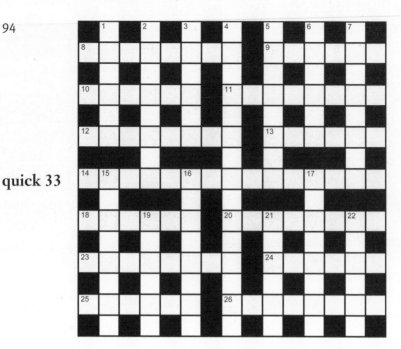

quick 33

Across

8 Indonesian islander, for example (8)
9 Uttar Pradesh market town, SE of Agra (6)
10 Part of Normandy or the Vendée typified by copses and hedgerows (6)
11 -------- Abbey, Nottinghamshire, England, home to Lord Byron (8)
12 Site of the world's largest flower auction in N Holland (8)
13 One of the two main islands that give their names to a Caribbean state (6)
14 Iranian uplands whose foothills provide most of the country's oil (6,9)
18 Aboriginals of central Australia (6)
20 Town in Oklahoma, originally the Wichita Indian Agency, the reservation for many eastern Native Americans (8)
23 Welsh town built on tinplate and cockles! (8)
24 Capital of Chechnya (variant spelling) (6)
25 Modern name for a 8 port, previously Bantam, which gave its name to the fowl (6)
26 Of people from an ancient part of Babylonia, home to Abraham (8)

Down

1 Ex-Indian princedom and city, now Vadodara (6)
2 Former name of Ujung Pandang, Indonesia (8)
3 Capital of Tigré Province, Ethiopia (6)
4 Rome's airport, alternatively named Fiumicino (8,2,5)
5 District of Canada's Northwest Territories now absorbed into Nunavut (8)
6 Latinized abbreviation for Cambridge (and University) (6)
7 Uzbek industrial city near the Kazakhstan and Kyrgyzstan borders (8)
15 Capital of the French department of Cantal (8)
16 State of Germany since 1959, following a plebiscite in 1935 (8)
17 N American town; S American monster! (8)
19 Samoyedic group of people living in forest and tundra regions north of the Urals (6)
21 Citizen of a S Asian Islamic republic (6)
22 Capital of the state of Perlis, NW Malaysia (6)

quick 34

Across

1 Mountains of S Australia (8,6)
10 Town of Alicante province, SE Spain, famed for its palm trees (5)
11 Bahamian island, Greek for 'freedom' (9)
12 Industrial town of Carinthia, S Austria (7)
13 Maori word for Mt Cook (7)
14 French town, capital of the Mayenne (5)
16 Proto-Arabian people, speakers of Aramaic (9)
19 Turkish province and its capital on the Dardanelles (9)
20 Scene of the siege in 1794 in which Nelson lost an eye (5)
22 Religion which takes the Granth as its scripture (7)
25 City of Thessaly, Greece, close to Mt Olympus (7)
27 Honshu industrial city, west of Osaka (9)
28 Former Tanganyikan town founded in 1927 with the discovery of gold (5)
29 La Manche, to the French (7,7)

Down

2 Largest body of fresh water in the Scottish lowlands (4,5)
3 Second city of Tabora Region, Tanzania (5)
4 Island in Mumbai harbour with four rock temples (9)
5 Tuscan city famed for its Palio horse races (5)
6 -------- Peninsula, which splits the Bellingshausen and Weddell Seas (9)
7 ----- Bay, inlet on Lake Superior (5)
8 One from an old German duchy whose heartland was Bavaria (7)
9 Market town of Somerset, England (6)
15 Body of water in N Finland, close to the Russian-Norwegian borders (4,5)
17 Rum-distilling town in Queensland (9)
18 Island forming the northernmost part of Nunavut (9)
19 Mountain range traversing Washington and Oregon states (7)
21 Nigeria's second city (6)
23 ----- Island, Iranian oil terminal in the in the Gulf (5)
24 Irish county, capital Navan (5)
26 Of a classical city said to have been founded in 735 BC (5)

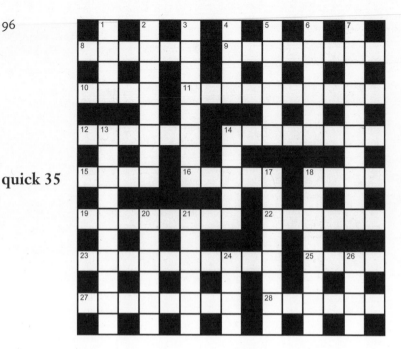

quick 35

Across

8 Jewish outpost besieged by Romans in 72 AD (6)
9 Former mining and railroad town of Nevada (3,5)
10 Italian city, famous for its 12th century campanile (4)
11 Algerian port since the 11th century (10)
12 The only landlocked region of Italy (6)
14 Town of Victoria, Australia, built on gold mining and wool (8)
15 Turkish city near the Syrian border, Edessa before 1637 (4)
16 ----- de Berre, large saltwater lagoon near the mouth of the Rhone (5)
18 Iranian region, capital Shiraz (4)
19 Industrial city of Ontario, capital of Upper Canada, 1841-44 (8)
22 Treaty of ------, 1802, ending the French Revolutionary Wars (6)
23 Federal States of ----------, capital Kolonia (10)
25 People of the Gold and Ivory Coast, of whom the Ashanti became most powerful in the 18th century (4)
27 Second city of Zimbabwe (8)
28 Tributary of the R Tagus in Spain with their confluence near Alcantara (6)

Down

1 German National Socialist (4)
2 Southernmost region of Italy, capital Reggio di -------- (8)
3 Californian city, the western gateway to the Mohave Desert (8)
4 Greek ruins, the 'holy land' which includes the Temple of Zeus at Olympia (4)
5 Nation formed originally after the death of Solomon (6)
6 River of the Urals which feeds the Kama and eventually the Volga (6)
7 Body of water in the Tanzanian arm of the Great Rift Valley, near Serengeti (4,6)
13 French Caribbean island (10)
14 Ancient province of the French Pyrenees (5)
17 W African (8)
18 Uttar Pradesh city, formerly the capital of the Oudh state (8)
20 Middle European (6)
21 One from the Friendly Islands, as was (6)
24 Caledonian (4)
26 Portuguese mountains, the western extension of the Serra da Estrela (4)

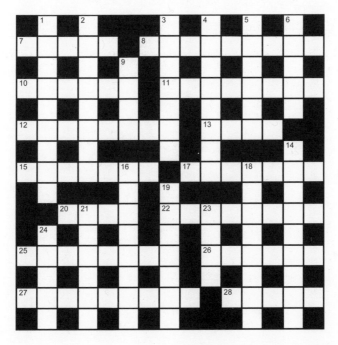

quick 36

Across

7 Barbadian (5)
8 Inlet in N Quebec (6,3)
10 Texan town on the Rio Grande, a Mexican border crossing (6)
11 Sea bound by Italy and the Balkan countries (8)
12 -------- (formerly Murchison) Falls on the Victoria Nile, Uganda (8)
13 City in Xinjiang Province, China, a 14th century Mongol capital (4)
15 Indonesian (i) (7)
17 Pre-Columbian ruins on the Yucatan Peninsula, Mexico (7)
20 Roman Aquae Sulis, in the English W Country (4)
22 One from a particular Balearic island (8)
25 Peloponnesian port (variant spelling) (8)
26 Israeli industrial city and Mediterranean resort (3,3)
27 Former mediaeval Armenian state, based on a modern Turkish city SE of Konya (9)
28 Sacred city and former capital of Sri Lanka (5)

Down

1 Environmentally important Ecuadorean islands (9)
2 City of Maharashtra at the confluence of the Girna and Masam rivers (8)
3 Iraqi city, popularly abbreviated, on the Euphrates R (2,5)
4 Ancient Irish kingdom, which through the Picts, spread to NW Scotland (8)
5 15 natives (6)
6 Pre-Columbian native American of the Lesser Antilles (5)
9 City in Guangxi Province, close to the borders of Yunnan Province and Vietnam (4)
14 Basque city, part of the Bilbao conurbation (variant spelling) (9)
16 Capital of Turkmenistan (variant spelling) (8)
18 Site of the Sikhs' holy Golden Temple (8)
19 Modern Ethiopian language, descended from Ge'ez (7)
21 Resting place of Noah's Ark after the Flood (6)
23 River of the Horn of Africa (4)
24 Indonesian (ii) (5)

quick 37

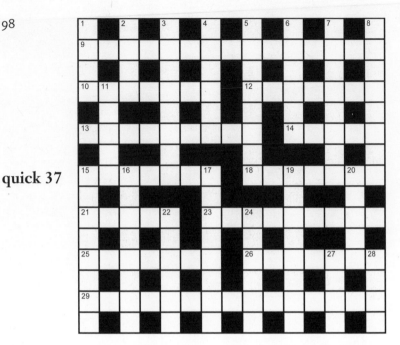

Across

9 Area of outstanding natural beauty in the Rockies, famed for its geysers (11,4)
10 Town in Madhya Pradesh, SE of Indore (7)
12 The Hoosier State, the 19th state of the Union (1816) (7)
13 Caucasian homeland of the Adyghe people, scattered after 19th century uprisings (9)
14 Texas agricultural and industrial town, north of Dallas (5)
15 Autonomous part of S central China, capital Yinchuan (7)
18 Lake fed mainly by the Amu Darya and Syr Darya rivers (4,3)
21 Cameroonian national park established in 1961 (5)
23 Lake District town associated with the Wordsworths and Matthew Arnold (9)
25 Western part of Czech Republic (7)
26 Island in the Bahamas, known for its aloe vera (7)
29 Inlet encompassing the Rhode I archipelago (12,3)

Down

1 Alaskan ski resort on the Copper R, named after a local people whose language is now officially dead (4)
2 Gaelic name for Scotland; Romanian region in Transylvania (4)
3 Capital of the French region of Aquitaine (8)
4 Those from a continent separated from others by the Urals and the Isthmus of Suez (6)
5 Honshu city SW of Fukushima (8)
6 English hills of Somerset (6)
7 4s from a country expanded into a federation in 1963 (8)
8 The Sooner State, the 46th of the Union (1907) (8)
11 Caribbean country, capital Port-au-Prince (5)
15 Danish port and largest town on Falster (8)
16 -------- Territory, self-governing member of the Commonwealth of Australia in 1978 (8)
17 One from Dixieland, for example (8)
19 Capital of Ogun State, Nigeria (8)
20 German North Sea port (5)
22 Grasslands of Argentina (6)
24 Siberian city on the Angara tributary of the Yenesei (6)
27 Nigerian people populating mainly the SE of the country (4)
28 Greek river of legend, the border with Hades (4)

quick 38

Across

6 Port at the head of the Mahanadi Delta, Orissa (7)
7 Port and resort in Dorset, England (5)
9 Hubei city on the shores of Lushui Reservoir (4)
10 --- - ------- Movement, created by the Havana Declaration, 1979 (3-7)
11 City and province of E Central Turkey (8)
13 Nomadic Berber of the Sahara (6)
15 French city, capital of the Tarn department (4)
17 ----- Heights, annexed by Israel after occupations in the Seven Days' and Yom Kippur Wars (5)
18 One of a Germanic race that sacked Rome in 410 AD (4)
19 One of the smallest of the Canary Islands (6)
20 Island off Venezuela visited by Columbus in 1498 (8)
23 Martinique volcano which erupted violently in 1902 (5,5)
26 Chinese river, longest in Inner Mongolia (4)
27 Ex-capital of Tigré, Ethiopia, where the Abyssinians routed the Italians in 1896 (5)
28 Valley near Jerusalem where Israelites sacrificed their own children: synonym for a place of torment (7)

Down

1 Border demarcating Greek and Turkish areas of Cyprus after 1974 (6,4)
2 Town in Emilia-Romagna which gives its name to richly coloured pottery (6)
3 W African peoples, including the Ashanti (4)
4 -------- Layer in the upper atmosphere which reflects short-wave radio waves to earth (8)
5 Minority nationality of S China (4)
6 Colombian river, the main tributary of the Magdalena (5)
8 Port of Washington State, N of Seattle on Puget Sound (7)
12 Belgian city's Carnival, which is typified by the 'throwing of the onions' (5)
14 Inhabitants of the most northern of the Leeward Is (10)
16 Mining centre in Andean Peru on the highest normal gauge railway in the world (2,5)
17 Scottish mountains (8)
21 Nigerian city, originally a centre of the slave trade (6)
22 Active volcanic peak (2542 m), one of the highest in Japan (5)
24 Greenland's capital, formerly Godthaab (4)
25 Old walled Galician city, E of Santiago de Compostela (4)

quick 39

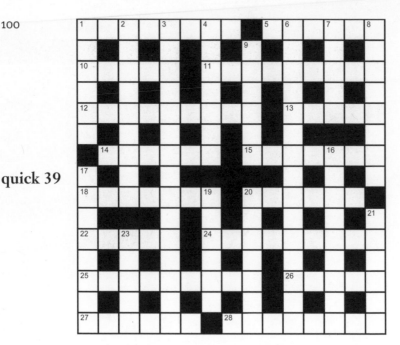

Across

1 Admiral Sir Francis -------, 1774-1857, British naval hydrographer (8)
5 Third-largest Greek island, home to the classical poet, Sappho (6)
10 France's longest river (5)
11 Scandinavian, independent since 1905 (9)
12 Native American mesa and its long-lived pueblo (5,4)
13 Capital of Vietnam (5)
14 Oklahoman town near the burial place of Geronimo and other Apaches (6)
15 Henan city on a northern tributary of the Yangtze (7)
18 ------- Transvaal, Mpumalanga since 1995 (7)
20 Texan river that empties into the Gulf of Mexico at Freeport (6)
22 The Gem State, the 43rd of the Union (1890) (5)
24 English county, the home of Windsor Castle and Ascot racecourse (9)
25 N Pacific archipelago (9)
26 Strict US Mennonite Christian sect (5)
27 Ecuadorean city, capital of the province of Imbabura (6)
28 Gnostic sect still surviving in Iraq and Iran (8)

Down

1 Ancient Finnish tribe which conquered lands near the Black Sea around the 7th century (6)
2 Citizens of part of SW USA (9)
3 Cooling sea breeze off the coast of Western Australia (9,6)
4 Capital of Burma (7)
6 Landmark in Mumbai harbour (9,6)
7 Heilongjiang Province border city, NE of Qiqihar (5)
8 Capital of Chile (8)
9 Myanmar west coast state, capital Sittwe (6)
16 Indigene, particularly associated with Australia (9)
17 Capital of Baja California State (8)
19 One from a part of Sudan or S Egypt (6)
20 Wine valley of S Australia (7)
21 Sichuan city, S of Chengdu, on the Yangtze R's Min tributary (6)
23 ---- culture, an ancient civilization of Ohio (5)

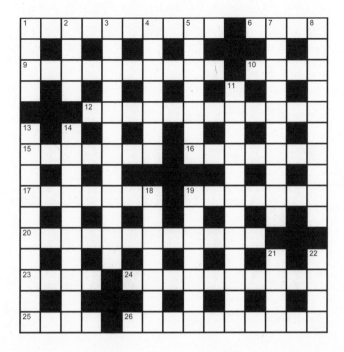

quick 40

Across

1 Resort region of Costa Rica, capital Liberia (10)
6 One from Latvia, Lithuania or Estonia (4)
9 Swedish industrial port near Malmo (10)
10 US Ivy League university (4)
12 Ski resort in Slovenia's Karawanken Alps (8,4)
15 Lake in an Italian volcano, the entrance to Hell in Roman mythology (7)
16 Highest mountain on the island of Rhodes (7)
17 Turkish department, and its capital, on the Black Sea (7)
19 Resort on the R Plate estuary in Uruguay (7)
20 Bavarian village which has held a Passion Play every decade since 1634 (12)
23 Capital of the Aisne department and of France between the 8th and 10th centuries (4)
24 Brazilian industrial city in the state of Minas Gerais (4,2,4)
25 Lough and river of Ireland (4)
26 Indigenous peoples of N Scandinavia (10)

Down

1 ---- Beach: a coastal town in Oregon; also, one of the D-Day landings (4)
2 Italian river which empties into the Ligurian Sea near Pisa (4)
3 Language family embracing peoples of SE Asia and Oceania (12)
4 Icelandic fishing port on Faxa Bay (7)
5 African country bordering the Mediterranean (7)
7 S Americans of Brazil, Venezuela, Colombia and Peru (10)
8 Familiar name for two US states which formed one territory before 1889 (3,7)
11 N region of Spain, capital Valladolid (8-4)
13 1d town of W Australia, at the end of the Nullarbor Plain (10)
14 Capital of Guyana (10)
18 Province, and its capital, of N Mozambique (7)
19 Belize town in a sugar-producing province on the Mexican border (7)
21 Former name of the Algerian port of Annaba (4)
22 Dutch river, rising in NE France as the Meuse (4)

quick 41

Across

7 Middle European (8)
8 State of N Brazil, capital Belém (4)
9 C African, in the Gulf of Guinea (8)
10 Ecuadorean river, the longest flowing west from the Andes (6)
11 Russian republic on the R Volga, capital Yoshkar-Ola (4,2)
12 Department of SE Turkey, and its capital (8)
13 Italian version of the largest city in that country outside of Rome (6)
14 People of SE India speaking the most widespread of the Dravidian tongues (6)
16 Town in Lincolnshire, England, home of the world's oldest air force training school (8)
19 India, as the Hindi-speakers name it (6)
21 Les ------, pine-backed coastal strip of Aquitaine (6)
22 Californian city, 'where the grass is greener'! (8)
23 Turkic Black Sea people, subdued by Charlemagne, 791-9 (4)
24 Brandy from Gascony (8)

Down

1 Nicaraguan department and its capital (6)
2 San Lorenzo de El --------, religious and royal complex NW of Madrid (8)
3 Residents of Kalaallit Nunaat (12)
4 Province and its capital in Basilicata region, S Italy (6)
5 Capital of Bahrain (6)
6 -------- -Wanganui, region of New Zealand/ Aotearoa (8)
10 W African country bordering Senegal (6-6)
13 Island group in the NW Pacific, capital Saipan (8)
15 Landlocked E Africans (8)
17 Gujarati city SE of Ahmadabad (6)
18 ------ Islands, a volcanic group off Italy, among which Stromboli is still active (6)
20 French alpine lake and city, capital of Haute-Savoie department (6)

quick 42

Across

7 Middle European (8)
8 State of N Brazil, capital Belém (4)
9 C African, in the Gulf of Guinea (8)
10 Ecuadorean river, the longest flowing west from the Andes (6)
11 Russian republic on the R Volga, capital Yoshkar-Ola (4,2)
12 Department of SE Turkey, and its capital (8)
13 Italian version of the largest city in that country outside of Rome (6)
14 People of SE India speaking the most widespread of the Dravidian tongues (6)
16 Town in Lincolnshire, England, home of the world's oldest air force training school (8)
19 India, as the Hindi-speakers name it (6)
21 Les ------, pine-backed coastal strip of Aquitaine (6)
22 Californian city, 'where the grass is greener'! (8)
23 Turkic Black Sea people, subdued by Charlemagne, 791-9 (4)
24 Brandy from Gascony (8)

Down

1 Nicaraguan department and its capital (6)
2 San Lorenzo de El --------, religious and royal complex NW of Madrid (8)
3 Residents of Kalaallit Nunaat (12)
4 Province and its capital in Basilicata region, S Italy (6)
5 Capital of Bahrain (6)
6 -------- -Wanganui, region of New Zealand/ Aotearoa (8)
10 W African country bordering Senegal (6-6)
13 Island group in the NW Pacific, capital Saipan (8)
15 Landlocked E Africans (8)
17 Gujarati city SE of Ahmadabad (6)
18 ------ Islands, a volcanic group off Italy, among which Stromboli is still active (6)
20 French alpine lake and city, capital of Haute-Savoie department (6)

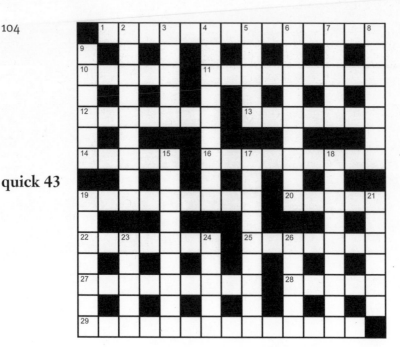

quick 43

Across

1 Atlantic island totally evacuated in 1961 because of volcanic activity (7,2,5)
10 The largest English ferry port (5)
11 Old name for Ciudad Bolivar in Venezuela and a tonic (9)
12 Sacred Indian river emptying into the Arabian Sea (7)
13 Shallow sea, north of Australia (7)
14 Scottish town, county town of Clackmannanshire of old (5)
16 German or Polish Jew (9)
19 Inhabitant of a Caribbean island invaded by the US in 1983 (9)
20 Jordan's only port (5)
22 Moravian city, now part of the Czech Republic (7)
25 Continental landmass extending from Cape Roca in the west to Cape Dezhnev in the east (7)
27 City near Braga, first capital of Portugal in the 12th century (9)
28 Zambia's commercial capital (5)
29 Massif of NE Algeria in the Sahara Atlas (5,9)

Down

2 European waterway (1159 km) to empty into the North Sea (5,4)
3 Modern country, once home to the Aramaeans (5)
4 Ruined Buddhist stupa in Andhra Pradesh; main tributary of the R Cauvery in Tamil Nadu (9)
5 Ghanaian national park on the banks of L Volta (5)
6 Californian city known for its boat building (5,4)
7 Pacific coral island republic, once rich in phosphates (5)
8 Pre-Pueblo SW USA culture, creators of the Basket Weaving period (7)
9 Polish Baltic port (6)
15 Algonquin Americans of modern-day SE USA (9)
17 See 18 (9)
18 Eventual name of the settlement on Pitcairn I, which administers 17 too (9)
19 The Peach State, one of the original 13 of the Union (7)
21 Capital of the autonomous Russian Federation Republic of Khakassia (6)
23 German city established as a Roman base by Augustus (5)
24 Islands which form a loose boomerang shape in the Bahamas (5)
26 Andalusian hill town, popular with tourists, on the R Guadalevin gorge (5)

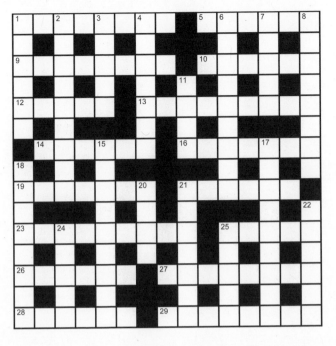

quick 44

Across
1 Sudanese region, capital El Obeid, split into three provinces in 1994 (8)
5 Language family of C Asia, including Turkic and Mongol (6)
9 Tunisian resort, on the Cap Bon peninsula (8)
10 Quebec peninsula, river and gulf (6)
12 Historic religious site and motor racing shrine of Milan (5)
13 Malawi before 1964 (9)
14 Inhabitants of Barbados (6)
16 Amazonian town in Colombia on the borders of Peru and Brazil (7)
19 ------- Caves, where palaeolithic paintings were discovered in 1940 (7)
21 African capital, formerly Salisbury (6)
23 Region of Botswana named after the endorheic basin irregularly fed by the Okavango delta (9)
25 World's largest diamond mine, in Botswana, in the heart of the Kalahari (5)
26 Uttar Pradesh market town on the R Yamuna (Jumna), prominent in the Indian Mutiny (1857) (6)
27 Of Italy's second city (8)
28 Once the single most productive cotton-spinning town in the world, in Greater Manchester (6)
29 Japanese industrial and engineering city SW of Tokyo (8)

Down
1 Capital of Nagaland state, NE India (6)
2 Citizens of a European country, 10% of whom are gypsies (9)
3 ----- Beach, the bloodiest of the Normandy landings on D-Day (5)
4 Entrance to Hell as seen in a crater lake NW of Naples? (7)
6 English royal house, whose monarchy began with the reign of Henry IV (1299) (9)
7 Honshu volcano close to Takasaki, last active in 1783 (5)
8 Relating to Aramaic-speaking people of biblical Babylonia (8)
11 Gaelic name for the Parliament of the Republic of Ireland (4)
15 Japanese 'gourmet' centre, the second city of Hokkaido (9)
17 Colombian seaport sacked by Drake in 1586 (9)
18 Region of S Portugal, capital Évora (8)
20 Capital of Shangxi province, one of twelve cities in China with over 3m inhabitants (4)
21 Largest port in Yemen (7)
22 Indian name for the Cauvery R (6)
24 Group of Finnish islands clustered at the mouth of the Gulf of Bothnia (5)
25 Almost the northernmost community in Honshu, on Shimokita peninsula, part of Mutsu City since 2005 (5)

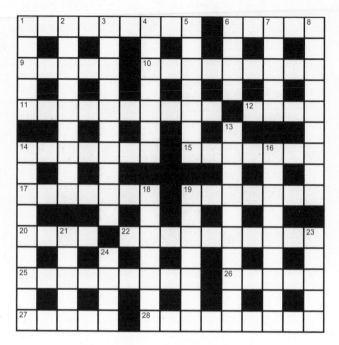

quick 45

Across

1 Italian name for the 9 road linking Rimini and Piacenza (3,6)
6 Mesoamerican people of the Gulf Coast, in Mexico (5)
9 Classical Italian (5)
10 Follower of a 2,000 year-old religion (9)
11 Peninsula in N Territory, Australia where aboriginals have lived for 40,000 years (6,4)
12 Port of Galicia, Spain (4)
14 Citizen of part of the US Midwest (7)
15 Most westerly state of the European Union (7)
17 So-called 'language isolate' of a region straddling the W Pyrenees (variant spelling) (7)
19 Ancient Indian kingdom reached in 326 BC by Alexander, who then turned back (7)
20 Four cities of the Sao Paolo conurbation known collectively by an acronym (4)
22 Scottish sporting resort near Auchterarder, Perthshire (10)
25 City of Bihar, India, NE of Patna (9)
26 Region of lakes, river valleys and glaciers in S Chile (5)
27 Panama's main port (5)
28 Turkish province and its capital, between Ankara and Istanbul (9)

Down

1 Bulgarian port and resort on the Black Sea (5)
2 Landlocked Caucasians (9)
3 Jamaican resort (7,3)
4 River in Australia, tributary of the Murrumbidgee (7)
5 Maori name for the highest peak in New Zealand (7)
6 French river and department, capital Beauvais (4)
7 River and port of Equatorial Guinea (5)
8 Argentinean port, on the Uruguay R (9)
13 Post-conquest region of NW S America (3,7)
14 Nordic character (9)
16 Region of S Spain dominated by the R Guadalquivir and the Sierra Nevada (9)
18 Capital of the US state of Georgia (7)
19 The Treasure State, the 41st state of the Union (1889) (7)
21 ----- Sea, part of the Pacific east of Australia (5)
23 Peninsula separating Asia and Africa (5)
24 Burmese hills close to the Indian border, highest peak Mt Victoria (3053 m) (4)

quick 46

Across

8 Main port in Equatorial Guinea (4)
9 Part of semi-desert uplands in S Africa between the Cape and the Orange R (5,5)
10 Danube river port developed by the Romans (6)
11 First city of Sardinia (8)
12 Eastern state of India, capital Kohima (8)
14 Islands of the Bahamas (6)
16 Kyushu port with ferry services to Honshu and Shikoku (4)
17 Port of Honshu, known for its August harvest Kanto festival (5)
18 Capital of Lower Normandy (4)
19 Capital of New Caledonia (6)
21 Third largest of the (English) Channel Is (8)
23 More general form of Buddhism, emphasizing the ideal of bodhisattva (8)
26 Former county town of Wiltshire, England, famed for its manufacture of quality carpets (6)
27 ---------- Bay, US Caribbean base (10)
28 S Turkish province, capital Mersin (4)

Down

1 Capital of Surinam (10)
2 Samoan unisex clothing (4-4)
3 Austro-Hungarian steppe-like grassland (6)
4 Acronym for the body that controls the flow and price of much of the world's oil (4)
5 Tocantins R tributary, flowing north for 2100 km (8)
6 Portuguese port and resort in the east of the Algarve (6)
7 Afrikaner pioneer (4)
13 Balkans river forming much of the Serbia-Bosnia border (5)
15 ---------- Swamp, Georgia-Florida national wildlife refuge (10)
17 Iranian city in the Zagros Mts between Bakhtaran and Hamadan (8)
18 Slavic alphabet (8)
20 The ------, lowland east of the Grampians, Scotland, the former county of Kincardineshire (6)
22 City in Yukon Territory, Canada, at the heart of the goldrush (6)
24 Province of the Dominican Republic and its capital (4)
25 N Ethiopian Cushtic dialect (4)

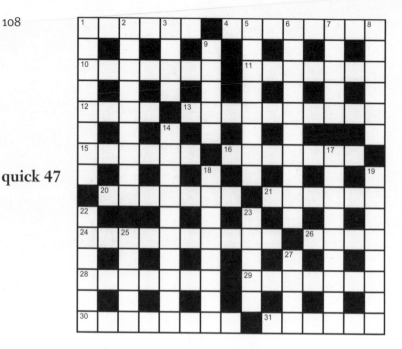

quick 47

Across

1 Historic, now heavily industrial Honshu city, NW of Kobe (6)
4 Warrior peoples of central India (8)
10 Chinese autonomous region traversed by the Great Wall (7)
11 Bulgarian industrial city, an important Ottoman craft centre (7)
12 The Beehive State, the 45th of the Union (4)
13 African country (1): capital Nouakchott (10)
15 Lake ------, forming part of the frontier between Dem Rep of Congo and 22 (6)
16 Caribbean republic, capital Kingston (7)
20 Largest town upriver from Córdoba on the R Guadalquivir (7)
21 Greek port and largest city of the Peloponnese (variant spelling) (6)
24 City of Rajasthan, NW of Delhi on the Pakistani border (10)
26 Syrian steel town, noted for its mediaeval water-wheel irrigation system (4)
28 Pygmy-like aboriginals of SE Asia (7)
29 African country (2): capital Ouagadougou (7)
30 Largest city of Aetolia-Acarnania, Greece (8)
31 World's second-largest country in area (6)

Down

1 C American citizen (8)
2 Capital of the Tarn-et-Garonne department, France (9)
3 City of Heilongjiang province, China, close to the Russian border (4)
5 Swedish river emptying into the Gulf of Bothnia at Harnosand (8)
6 Pakistani resort of the 19, named after a British army officer (10)
7 Dutch town after which the southernmost point of S America was named (5)
8 Citizen, since 1993, of a fully independent European state (6)
9 Gujarati city east of the Rann of Kutch (5)
14 Native American of the S Andes (10)
17 City of Espírito Santo province, Brazil, near Vitoria (9)
18 Largest city of San Martín region, Peru, a stop-off point for Andes and Amazon tours (8)
19 Region of the world's highest mountains (8)
22 African country (3): capital Kampala (6)
23 Sumatran city, NW of Palambang (5)
25 African country (4): capital Niamey (5)
27 Greek province and its capital (4)

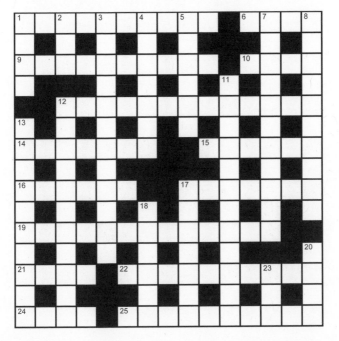

quick 48

Across

1 Citizen of the largest city in Scotland (10)
6 Capital of Samoa (4)
9 Maharashtra textile town, formerly a 17th century Mogul capital (10)
10 ---- Loch, US Navy's Scottish base for Polaris missile submarines, 1960-92 (4)
12 Lancashire twin resort, linked by 'and' when referring to the championship golf links there (6,2,5)
14 Baltic country, capital Tallinn (7)
15 Mexican resort on the Caribbean (6)
16 Uprising of mainly 18 people against the British in Kenya, 1952-60 (3,3)
17 S American desert (7)
19 Alternative name for the Ryukyu Archipelago (6,7)
21 Scottish W coast fishing and ferry port (4)
22 Inhabitant of a region in the centre of France (10)
24 Scottish loch occupying part of Glen More (Great Glen) (4)
25 E Europeans descended from migrant Finns in the 7th century (10)

Down

1 Pacific island state, an 'unincorporated territory' of the USA, capital Agaña (4)
2 German river valley, the northernmost commercially viable vine-growing area in Europe (3)
3 N Carolina town, dubbed 'Camel City', due to its tobacco industry (7-5)
4 Former Moorish capital in Andalucia (7)
5 Ethiopian rift valley lake (variant spelling) (6)
7 Descendants of Canaanites, great traders of the Mediterranean in ancient times (11)
8 Ethiopian, of old (10)
11 District of Pakistani Punjab, bounded to the north by the R Sutlej, and its capital (12)
12 Independent Baltic peoples, often in the past in the sway of Poland or Russia (11)
13 City in Ohio settled by middle-Europeans and site of a Revolutionary War battle in 1777 (10)
17 Austrian pass, the sole road/rail link to the Tyrol from the west (7)
18 Largest Bantu-speaking people of Kenya (6)
20 Name given to the R Thames in the Oxford area (4)
23 Honshu city, NW of Tokyo (3)

quick 49

Across

7 Well-to-do Los Angeles suburb (3,3)
8 Saharan oasis town in Libya (8)
9 Port and resort of Cyprus (8)
10 Dutch Rhine town, NE of Rotterdam (6)
11 Peruvian city, capital of Lambayeque department (8)
12 Huge iron and steel city of Liaoning province, China (6)
13 City and district of Uttar Pradesh, on the R Ganges (11)
18 Ancient Malaysian trading port, now a resort city (6)
20 One of the original 13 counties of Wales, now a part of Gwynedd (8)
22 The ------, the southernmost part of England (6)
23 French region, a former kingdom, the provider of some of the world's greatest wines (8)
24 Town close to a famous Riviera resort of a similar name (2,6)
25 Italy's third city (6)

Down

1 Biblical oasis town in Palestine, near the Dead Sea (7)
2 Flat dry area of SE Spain (2,6)
3 State of India, capital Bhubaneswar (6)
4 Honshu industrial city with ferry links to Shikoku (8)
5 Brazilian city in the state of Rio de Janeiro known for its sugar- and petroleum-linked industries (6)
6 Abbey near Dijon founded in 1098, now occupied by Trappist monks (7)
8 Inlet north of Mumbai formerly known as Cambay (4,2,7)
14 Citizens of a C African state (8)
15 Department and its capital, an Andean oasis city of S Peru (8)
16 Town of Wiltshire, England, besieged by Parliamentary forces in 1643 (7)
17 The -------, a series of sea stacks off the west coast of the Isle of Wight, England (7)
19 Oil-refining port of Iran's Shatt al-Arab (6)
21 Catalonian city whose airport was the original gateway to the Costa Brava resorts (variant spelling) (6)

quick 50

Across

5 Gang or Shuli linguistic group of N Uganda/S Sudan (6)
7 Botswana river and swampland (8)
9 Bulgaria's first purpose-built Black Sea holiday resort (8)
10 City and province of NW Turkey (6)
11 Legendary, symbolic boulder in New England, associated with the Pilgrim Fathers (8,4)
13 Capital of Liguria, Italy (variant spelling) (6)
15 German river which joins the Rhine at Mannheim (6)
18 Colombian port, and the first air terminal in S America (12)
21 Almost landlocked N European sea (6)
22 Of Atlantic islands midway between Norway and Iceland (8)
23 Hubei city on the Han R, NW of Wuhan (8)
24 Devon cathedral city, Roman Isca (6)

Down

1 Port of C Chile (8)
2 Second Hindu god of the triad (6)
3 Legislative capital of the Republic of South Africa (4,4)
4 Scottish town, the largest in Borders Region (6)
6 Part of the SW Pacific administered by Australia (5,3)
7 Industrial city of NE Kansas, in the Kansas City conurbation (6)
8 Largest group of people in C India (4)
12 County town of Cumbria, England (8)
14 Sea and airport for the Canary I of Lanzarote (8)
16 Massachusetts town on the Connecticut R, at its confluence with a river of the same name (8)
17 World's fifth-largest island (6)
18 Bay in Australia named in 1770 after a study by Sir Joseph Banks (6)
19 *La belle province* of Canada (6)
20 Indonesian holiday island (4)

CROSSWORD SOLUTIONS
AND CRYPTIC EXPLANATIONS

1

EXPLANATIONS

Across: 1 Bra+h+MA, **4** Tomb+anag of 'solo',
9 Anag, **11** T(-r)ay+side, **12** E+kin [rev] & pun,
13 Sien(-n)a, **14** V(oz)A [all rev], **17** Anag of
'oars' around G+a+SS, **18** Anag of 'Sargas
(-anag of 'sso'), **20** Double def [ref former
Ecuadorean currency], **22** IR+o+quo+is & pun,
26 Pun, **27** Fund+y, **28** Homophone of 'fear',
30 Double def & pun of the two Londons,
32 (-As)Syrians, **33** Key+largo, **34** Pun.
Down: 1 B+anag of 'rants' about 'E', **2** AB+ou+kir,
3 M(A)u(1), **5** O+anag of 'nest'+d, **6** Double
def, **7** Le(1+anag of 'zip')g, **8** Pun, **10** Ici+
(-r)est, **15** Reversed hidden word in 'saLES
ABout', **16** IRA+IQ [rev], **19** Double def & pun ,
20 Anag of 'as war'+a+K, **21** Cock+yen [rev],
23 Anag, **24** 'St' [rev] in 'Sure'+y, **25** Tu(are)g,
29 A+RN+o, **31** Double def & pun.

2

T	H	E	S	S	A	L	Y		B	A	S	R	A
H		A		L		L		O		I		H	N
A	A	L	B	O	R	G		R	E	A	D	I	N	G
S		A		V		O		U		F		K	U
S	E	L	M	A		A	L	B	E	R	T	A	N	S
O			K		B		A		A		A		R
C	H	I	S	I	N	A	U			I	P	O	H
K		C		A		Y		M		A		U	A
S	U	E	Z			B	I	S	M	A	R	C	K
	L		P		T		Y		R				O
G	U	A	T	E	M	A	L	A		A	K	K	A	D
O		N		O		O		Z		V		U	A
M	A	D	U	R	A	I		A	L	A	C	A	N	T
E		E		I		S		K		T		L	E
L	O	R	C	A		T	R	I	N	I	D	A	D

EXPLANATIONS

Across: 1 T+he(lass[rev])y, **6** B(AS[rev])ra,
10 AA+l+Borg, **11** Double def, **12** S(elm)a,
13 Albert+ans & pun, **14** Anag of 'Sichuan'
around '1', **16** Hopi[rev], **20** Sue+z, **21** Double
def & pun, **24** Gua(ET[rev])m+a+la,
25 A+KK+ad, **27** Mad+u+RAI, **28** A la+cant,
29 Anag, **30** Tri(din[rev])ad.
Down: 2 Hal+a+L, **3** Homophone of 'Czechs' &
pun, **4** Al+go+a+bay, **5** Roy[rev]+U+BA,
6 B(anag of 'fair')A, **7** Anag of 'UK parish'
around 'R', **8** An+Gus, **9** Has+socks,
15 Homophone of 'I slander' & pun on my
pseudonym, **17** Anag of 'Hokkaido' minus '1' &
'K'+Te, **18** Anag of 'mazy Kia' +I,
19 Am(Rav[-i])ati, **22** PE+O+anag of 'air',
23 Taois(-each)+t, **24** Go+mel,
26 K(U)ala(-hari).

3

```
E V E R E S T ■ T R I O L E T
T ■ L ■ R ■ U ■ O ■ N ■ E ■ O
R O M A N I A ■ N I C O B A R
U ■ I ■ E ■ R ■ G ■ A ■ A ■ R
R E N O ■ J E H A D ■ K N E E
I ■ Y ■ T ■ G ■ N ■ S ■ O ■ O
A V A T A R S ■ S H A N N O N
■ ■ ■ J ■ ■ ■ ■ ■ L ■ ■ ■ ■ ■
K U W A I T I ■ S E E L A N D
A ■ O ■ K ■ N ■ I ■ M ■ T ■ E
S A U D ■ A D R A R ■ Y A L E
H ■ N ■ F ■ I ■ M ■ A ■ C ■ S
M A D E I R A ■ E U S K A D I
I ■ E ■ N ■ N ■ S ■ T ■ M ■ D
R E D O N D A ■ E M I R A T E
```

EXPLANATIONS

Across: 1 Eve+rest & pun, **5** Double def, **9** R(Omani)a & pun on vampires, **10** 'Cob' in 'rain' [rev], **11** Loner or (l-oner[rev]), **12** Je+h+ad, **16** Anag, **17** Sh+an(N)on, **18** Homophone of 'Queue'+wait+I, **21** See+land, **24** Hidden word in 'NasSAU District', **25** A+d+rar(-e), **26** Double def & pun, **29** Made+IRA, **30** Anag, **31** Re(don)d+A, **32** ETA+rime[rev].

Down: 1 Anag of 'true'+air[rev], **2** Elm+in+y+a, **3** Double def (ref Lough Erne), **4** (+S)+tuar(-t)+eg(-S), **5** Tong(an)s, **6** Anag of (-Amer)ican, **7** 'Ban' in 'Noel' [rev], **8** Tor(anag of 'ore')n, **14** Taj+1+K, **15** Double def [ref Salem witch trials of 1692], **18** Homophone of 'cash'+'mere', **19/13** Pun, **20** IN+Diana, **21** Anag, **22** A+t+a+C+a+MA, **23** Homophone of 'D'+side, **27** Fin+n, **28** A(St)1.

4

```
■ C A R D I F F ■ A S M A R A
■ U ■ O ■ S ■ R ■ Y ■ A ■ O ■
O M A N ■ E F A T E ■ R O S S
■ B ■ D ■ R ■ N ■ R ■ A ■ A ■
G R E A T L A K E S ■ C O R K
■ I ■ ■ O ■ F ■ ■ ■ A ■ I ■
Z A R D E H K U H ■ D I J O N
■ A ■ N ■ R ■ B ■ B ■ ■ ■ ■
T U L L E ■ S T O R N O W A Y
■ P ■ M ■ A ■ A ■ ■ ■ B ■
A P I A ■ J A M S H E D P U R
■ S ■ T ■ A ■ M ■ M ■ H ■ M ■
W A D I ■ P R A I A ■ A M U R
■ L ■ A ■ A ■ I ■ N ■ K ■ S ■
H A I N A N ■ N I I G A T A
```

EXPLANATIONS

Across: 1 Car+Di+ff, **5** A+S(ram[rev])A, **8** O+man, **9** E+fate, **10** Homophone of 'sea', **11** Anag, **12** Double def, **13** Anag of 'herd Kazakh' minus 'a'+'K' around 'U', **15** Double def & pun, **17** Hidden word reversed in 'wELL UTilized' linked & to previous def, **19** St+OR+no way, **21** A(pi)A, **22** Anag, **24** Pun, **25** P(RAI)A, **26** A+rum[rev], **27** H(A+in)an, **28** Anag.

Down: 1 Cu+MB+air[rev], **2** R(-H)ond(-D)a, **3** Anag of 'Rhine los(-t)', **4** Anag of 'affirm+tank'+am, **5** Pun, **6** Anag, **7** Anag of 'soar'+Rio, **14** Double def, **16** Bra+H(man)i, **18** U(pp)S+a la, **20** A+bum+USA, **22** Ja(PA)n, **23** D+haka.

5

```
S I T T I N G B O U R N E ■ ■
■ T ■ H ■ A ■ A ■ L ■ U ■ E
S A G A R M A T H A ■ K A N O
■ L ■ I ■ P ■ A ■ N ■ U ■ G
W I N S L O W ■ ■ B R A I L A
■ A ■ ■ B ■ A ■ L ■ I ■
A N A T O L I A ■ T S O T S I
■ R ■ I ■ O ■ N ■ O ■ F ■ H
H I N D U S ■ T O R R A N C E
■ V ■ A ■ M ■ U ■ ■ ■ H ■
R I A L T O ■ ■ I B E R I A N
■ E ■ W ■ C ■ G ■ R ■ A ■ N
U R F A ■ H E L L E S P O N T
■ A ■ V ■ I ■ E ■ D ■ I ■ E
■ N E L S O N M A N D E L A ■
```

EXPLANATIONS

Across: 1 Sitting+Bourne, **9** Anag+a, **10** K+a+no, **11** Wins+low, **12** BR+A(-ustri)(1+L)A, **14** A(NATO)lia, **17** Anag, **18** Hind+US, **19** Homophone of 'torrents', **20** Rial+to, **21** (-T)Iberian, **25** Hidden word in 'ResURFAcing', **26** Anag, **27** Nelson+man+de la.

Down: 2 Italian+(1+vir[rev])+era, **3** Th(A)is, **4** N(amp)o, **5** Rev initial letters, **6** Anag, **7** Anag of 'a foul UK' in 'Na', **8** Pun on 'Le Manche', **13** Ban+TU, **15** Compound anag of 'Latvia' and 'Wed', **16** Los(Moch[-a+i{-t}])s, **22** Br(-i)e+ad[rev], **23** Double def & pun, **24** Double def.

6

EXPLANATIONS
Across: 1 B(ale)ar+I/C, **5** Par+see, **9** Ran+c+agua, **10** Afar+S, **12** U(lur[-e])U & pun on alternative to Ayers Rock, **13** Anag, **14** Hidden word in 'AmericAN DESert' & lit, **16** Mexic(-o)+Ali, **19** Double def & pun, **20** Anag of 'lignite' minus 'it', **22** Armo(-u)r+i+can, **24** Naive[rev], **25** O+r[rev] in odd letters, g+o+t, **26** Ram's+gate, **27** Ride[rev]+NE, **28** Ja+anag of 'insist'.
Down: 1 Anag & lit/pun, **2** Lang+U+code[rev], **3** Hidden word in 'heAT A FUmarole', **4** Composite anag of 'ungracious' minus 'Rons', **6** Double def & pun on Asia Minor, **7** S(n)ake, **8** Anag, **11** D(-air)y+fed, **15** Sa(1+ram[rev]tan, **17** Anag & lit, **18** Double def, **21** Homophone of 'anchor'+a, **23** Ma(or)i, **24** Essen(-e).

7

EXPLANATIONS
Across: 1 Double def & pun, **4** 1+bar+(-s)aki, **8** Dot+Han, **9** Anag of 'train' in O & O, **12** Pun on Lady B from 'The Importance of being Ernest', **13** Anag of 'British' minus 'BT', **14** Le(H+anag of 'Var')e, **15** D(a+pug[rev])an, **17** B(ENG)ali, **19** Sole+dad, **21** Es+poo!, **23** Anag of 'Noble Rhine' minus 'E', **24** F(UK)u+OK+a, **25** In(-t)uit+s & lit, **26** AS(a+race)N, **27** Double def and pun.
Down: 1 Anag of 'bribes'+'disable' minus 'r'+s, **2** Double def & pun, **3** K+hark+IV=four [o'clock], **5** Anag of 'sad Belgians' around 'H', **6** Double def, **7** K(ail)1, **10** Anag, **11** Ching(-Ford)+d(-irt)y+nasty, **16** Po(d)go+Rica, **18** A+Co+run+a, **20** Lu(BA)ng+o, **22** Pi+Ur+a.

8

EXPLANATIONS
Across: 1/18/2 Anag, **9** Double def & pun on definite article, **10** Et+rur(I)a(-l), **11** Anag, **12** Pun, **13** A+sun+c(1)on, **15** Anag of '1+has', **20** d+old rums, **24** Anag, **26** Ran[rev](y)+N, **27** Abe+anag on 'akin', **28** Double def & pun on Andres S, famous 20thC guitarist, **29** Fort+[Harry] Lauder+dale.
Down: 1 F(U)ling, **3** Anag, **4** Double def, **5** Double def & Pun, **6** Homophones of 'Swede' & 'Dick' after nor, **7** Turk+(-d)ish, **8** Bag+h+dad, **14** In+do+china, **16** Saw+bijo(-u) [all rev], **17** Sr+in anag of 'raga', **19** Henge+lo, **21** Hidden word in 'treMOR AVIAtor', **22** Havan(-a)+t, **23** Un+1+ate, **25** Has+ID.

9

```
B I S M A R C K ■ U G A N D A
O ■ A ■ L ■ O ■ ■ A A ■ ■ C
M E M S A H I B ■ O R A D E A
B ■ A ■ I ■ M I ■ I ■ ■ O ■ P
A R R A N ■ B A B A B U R N U
Y ■ K ■ R ■ R A ■ ■ ■ ■ ■ L
■ N A G O Y A ■ I S L A M I C
S ■ N ■ S ■ ■ D ■ I ■ ■ O
R E D O N D A ■ C A I R N S ■
I ■ A ■ L ■ A ■ ■ N ■ ■ T
L E S A B Y M E S ■ S I E N A
A ■ A ■ R ■ A T ■ E ■ ■ S ■ R
N A B L U S ■ L I E G E O I S
K ■ R ■ C ■ ■ L ■ O ■ ■ T ■ U
A L A S K A ■ B E A U V A I S
```

EXPLANATIONS

Across: 1 Anag of 'bricks' around 'am',
5 U(GA)nd+A, **9** Anag of 'sham+MBE' around
'1', **10** Hidden word in 'sponsOR A DEAl',
12 (-B)arra(N), **13** Baba+burn+U,
14 n+a+Goya, **16** Anag of 'calm is' around 'I',
19 Re+don+ad[rev], **21** Double def,
23 Le & anag of 'embassy', **25** S(1)+E+N+a,
26 Nab+L+US, **27** Anag, **28** Al(ask)a,
29 Baeu(V+A1)s.
Down: 1 Bomb+a+y, **2** S(a+mark)and, **3** Al ain,
4 Hidden word in 'ZiCO IM BRAzilian',
6 Pun, **7** N(-igeria)a+rod[rev], **8** A cap
(u[-nsuccessfu]l)+Co, **11** Initial letters, **15** Anag,
17 Mi(n)nes+OT+a, **18** Pun on former island's
name 'Serendip', **20** (-f)al(-l)+MA [ref battle in
the Crimean War, 1854], **21** Cast+anag of 'lie',
22 Tars+US, **24** SA+bra, **25** S+eg+OU.

10

```
B E C H U A N A L A N D ■
Y ■ H ■ L ■ A ■ A ■ I ■ D A
B R U N S W I C K ■ G H E N T
L ■ P ■ T ■ R ■ E ■ E ■ L ■
O H A R E ■ A N T A R C T I C
S ■ N ■ R ■ ■ S ■ I ■ A ■ A
■ ■ P A N A R A B I S M
S ■ A ■ H ■ P ■ N ■ N ■ C ■
P U N T A R E N A S ■
O ■ D ■ N ■ N ■ L ■ V ■ D
K A R A G A N D A ■ E F A T E
A ■ E ■ Z ■ I ■ S ■ V ■ N ■ S
N E A T H ■ N E W C A S T L E
E ■ S ■ O ■ E ■ A ■ N ■ A ■ R
■ H U D S O N S T R A I T
```

EXPLANATIONS

Across: 1 Anag, **9** Pun, **10** G(hen)T, **11** O+hare,
12 Anag of 'cart in 'antic', **13** Pan+a(Rab[-
B]is)m, **18** Punt(-A)arenas, **22** Kara+
homophone of 'gander', **24** E+fat+E,
25 Anag of '(-he)athen', **26** Pun, **27** [Rock]
Hudson's trait.
Down: 1 Anag, **2** Hidden word in 'FrenCH
UPANishad', **3** Double def & pun of garment
so named, **4** (-Nige)+anag of 'rian'+a,
5 Anag, ref orig name of L Tana, **6** Niger+Ian,
7 Delta+I+C, **8/21** A+t+homophone of
'a+calmer'+desert, **14** A+pen(nine)s,
15 Spok(a+n)e, **16** (-San) Andreas & pun,
17 Hang+Zhou, **19** Homophone of 'le+vin'+t,
20 VA+n't+AA, **23** A+swan.

11

```
L A K E T I T I C A C A
A ■ U ■ O ■ R ■ O ■ E ■ F G
S L O V A K I A N ■ L U O H E
H ■ P ■ M ■ E ■ A ■ T ■ R ■ O
I B I Z A N S ■ K A S H M I R
O ■ O ■ S ■ T ■ R ■ ■ O ■ G
■ R I V E R Y E N I S E I
A ■ S ■ N ■ ■ G ■ A ■ A
G U A N A B A R A B A Y ■
U ■ R ■ R ■ I ■ M ■ G ■ B
L A A L A N D ■ R A I N I E R
H ■ W ■ L ■ E ■ D ■ L ■ T ■ O
A D A N A ■ C A R T A G E N A
S ■ K ■ V ■ H ■ I ■ N ■ G ■ D
■ C A P E V E R D E A N S
```

EXPLANATIONS

Across: 1 Anag & pun , **9** Homophone of 'Czech'
& pun on Velvet Divorce, **10** Anag of U' +
'hole', **11** Ib(-ER)i(+Z)ans, **12** Homophone of
'cash'+mere', **13** Anag of 'vineries' and 'rye'+1,
17 Anag of 'a+gun'+a+bar+a+bay,
22 La+A+land, **24** Double def, **25** A+dan+a,
26 Cart+a+gen(-t)+a, **27** Anag .
Down: 3 To+amas(-s)+in+A, **4** Tries+t(-im)e,
5 Con(a)k+Ry, **6** Anag, **7** For+anag of Ma(s)o,
8 Pun on the song, **14** ng+a+mil+anag of 'Dan',
15 A+gul(-l)+has, **16** Anag of 'as war'+a+K,
18 Double def & pun on the Ardèche gorges,
19 (-H)Airdrie(-r), **20** G(I+te)G+a,
23 A+val+A[all rev].

12

```
E L L I C E ■ A S W A N D A M
A ■ A ■ O ■ A ■ A ■ U ■ O ■ I
S A H A R A N ■ M A G A D A N
T ■ T ■ O ■ D ■ O ■ U ■ G ■ S
T A I A N ■ A D A M S P E A K
I ■ ■ E ■ M ■ N ■ T ■ C ■ ■
M A G E L L A N ■ ■ A R I C A
O ■ R ■ ■ N ■ P ■ ■ ■ T ■ L
R H E I N ■ ■ B L A N T Y R E
■ A ■ D ■ S ■ A ■ I ■ ■ ■ U
H O T T E N T O T ■ I N U I T
A ■ G ■ B ■ A ■ E ■ G ■ R ■ I
G I L B E R T ■ A D A M A W A
E ■ E ■ L ■ E ■ U ■ T ■ W ■ N
N A N K E E N S ■ C A L A I S
```

EXPLANATIONS

Across: 4 Anag of 'Andawa'+S+N minus 'a', 10 Has[rev]+Aran, 11 MA+GA+dan, 12 T(A)i(A)n, 13 Adam+speak, 14 Homophone of 'straight' & pun on narrow=strait, 16 A(-f)rica, 19 Rhein[-gold], 21 Anag of 'by Lear' around NT, 24 Hot+tent+OT, 25 1+nuit, 27&1 [WS] Gilbert+ell+ice, 28 Adam+a+WA, 29 Nan(keen)'s, 30 CA+anag of 'sial'.

Down: 1 Anag & lit, 2 Hidden word in 'MulLAH TIght-lipped', 3 Cor(on)e+l, 5 SA+moan, 6 August+a, 7 Dodge+City & pun, 8 Min(s)k, 9 'N'+anag of 'Aswan Dam' minus 'S+W', 15 Double def & pun on alternative name 'Glen More', 17 Anag, 18 Double def, 20 Anag, 22 Anag, 23 State+N, 24 H+a+gen, 26 A+war+U [all rev].

13

```
E U S K A R A ■ A N T I G U A
L ■ W ■ L ■ C ■ N ■ H ■ I ■ N
M I A S S ■ H Y D E R A B A D
I ■ Z ■ A ■ E ■ C ■ A ■ R ■ O
S T I L T O N ■ A L K M A A R
T ■ ■ I ■ ■ I ■ ■ I ■ L ■ ■ R
I C E L A N D I C ■ ■ E T N A
■ A ■ N ■ U ■ O ■ T ■ A ■ ■
B A S S ■ B O S P H O R U S
U ■ T ■ X ■ R ■ ■ R ■ ■ ■ A
K O L P I N O ■ T R I P O L I
H ■ E ■ A ■ V ■ U ■ S ■ M ■ N
A S I A M I N O R ■ S H A T T
R ■ G ■ E ■ I ■ K ■ U ■ H ■ E
A C H I N S K ■ S Y R I A N S
```

EXPLANATIONS

Across: 1 EU+Araks [rev] [ref R Araks valley claimed to be the biblical G of E], 5 Hidden word in 'giANT IGUAnas', 9 M(1)ass, 10 Anag & pun on the princedom of the Nizams, 11 Stilt+on, 12 'La' [rev]+anag of 'maarkt', 13 Ic(eland)i+C, 16 Ante (rev) & pun on the highest volcano in Europe, 18 Homophone & pun, 19 As previous clue, 22 Anag, 23 Trip+anag of 'oil', 25 Asia+minor, 26 Sh+att(-ack), 27 A+Ch+in+S(-molens)k, 28 (-As)Syrians & pun.

Down: 1 El(mist)i, 2 S+W+a+Z+I, 3 Double def, 4 A(-a)chen, 6 Anag, 7 Double def & homophone of 'monkeys'/barbary apes pun, 8 And/or+ hidden word in 'fRAnce' & lit, 14 East+(-RA)leigh, 15 Anag of Kurd+bovin(-e), 17 Th(R)is+sur, 18 UK+H in anag of 'Arab', 20 Saint(E)s, 21 XI+Amen, 23/5 Turks+anag of 'no cicadas', 24 A+ham+o [all rev].

14

```
H E L W A N ■ W A R A N G A L
E ■ A ■ V ■ M ■ N ■ R ■ O ■ A
B E N D I G O ■ Y U A N L I N
R ■ A ■ G ■ M ■ A ■ P ■ D ■ Z
E V I A N ■ B A N D A A C E H
W ■ ■ O ■ A ■ G ■ H ■ O ■ O
S U D A N E S E ■ ■ O T A R U
■ U ■ ■ A ■ B ■ ■ ■ S ■ ■
J A M B I ■ P A K I S T A N
A ■ A ■ C ■ D ■ N ■ B ■ ■ O
M A G D E B U R G ■ E I G E R
A ■ U ■ L ■ N ■ K ■ R ■ A ■ M
I R E L A N D ■ O N I T S H A
C ■ T ■ N ■ E ■ K ■ A ■ P ■ N
A B E R D E E N ■ A N G E R S
```

EXPLANATIONS

Across: 1 Hel(-l)+wan, 4 War+a+n+gal, 10 Bend+1+go, 11 Yuan+nil [rev], 12 E(via)N, 13 [Hastings] Banda+ace+H, 14 Su(Danes)e, 16 O+tar+U, 18 Jam+B+1, 20 Pa(K+1)sta+n, 24 Anag of 'Bermuda' with 'G+G', 25 E(i)g+re [rev], 27 Ire+land, 28 Anag, 29 A(anag of 'breed'+E)n 30 Double def.

Down: 1 Double def & pun, 2 Hidden word in 'MagelLAN Almed', 3 A(VI+G)non, 5 An(-d)+yang [ref to ancient capital of Yin {or Shang} Dynasty of the same name], 6 A+rap+a+ho, 7 Anag, 8 La+n+zho+U, 9 Mo(m)b+a+SA, 15 Anag of 'Te Deum' about anag of 'Aug', 17 Ban(G+[OK, rev])k, 18 Jam+a+anag of 'CIA', 19 Ice+land, 21 (-S)Iberian, 22 Norm+ans, 23 Dun+Dee, 26 EP+sag [all rev].

15

L	U	D	W	I	G	S	H	A	F	E	N		
I		U		M		T		Z		L		D	I
N	E	L	S	P	R	U	I	T		B	E	N	I	N
H		U		E		T		E		E		I		S
A	N	T	A	R	C	T	I	C	A		L	E	N	A
I		H		A		G			C		P		L
		S	T	R	A	I	T		A	D	E	N	A
A		A		R		R		U		M		R		H
F	A	R	S	I		T	A	R	T	A	R	
R		C		Z			R		R		L		G
I	R	A	Q		A	D	D	I	S	A	B	A	B	A
C		D		M		O		A		G		M		L
A	R	I	C	A		V	A	L	D	I	S	E	R	E
N		A		L		E		B		B		S		N
		S	I	E	R	R	A	N	E	V	A	D	A

EXPLANATIONS
Across: 1 Ludwig's+ha(-V+f)en, 9 Anag, 10 Beni(-G)n, 11 Anag, 12 Double def, 16 A+den+a, 19 Far+is [rev], 20 Tar+tar, 23 Ira+Q, 24 (-C)Addis+A+BA+BA, 27 A(-f)rica(-n), 28 Anag of 'pearl divers' minus 'P'+'R', 29 Double def & pun on ranges with the same name.
Down: 1 Hidden word in 'CanaL IN HAIning', 2 Du+Luth(-eran), 3 Anag, 4 Stutt(-er)+gart(-er), 5 AZ+'tec, 6 E(lb)E, 7 Anag of 'ephedrine' minus 'h'+'E', 8 Ins(-h)al(-l)ah, 13 Anag, 15 T(Ur)rial+BA, 17 Double def & pun on John Huston's 1951 classic, 18 A(R)cadia, 21 Double def & pun, 22 Gale+N(-ebrask)a [ref base for 18th C pioneers], 25/14 Pun, 26 Initial letters.

16

	K	H	O	N	K	A	E	N		T	A	T	A	R
P		A		O		R		A		O		I		A
E	R	I	T	R	E	A		S	A	L	A	M	I	S
R		T		T		W		H		U		B		H
I	R	I	S	H		A	G	I	N	C	O	U	R	T
G			E		K		K		A		C		
O	M	D	U	R	M	A	N			E	T	N	A
R		A		N		N		D		A		O		L
D	I	S	S			P	E	M	B	R	O	K	E
	H		H		B		M		E				U
A	N	T	S	I	R	A	B	E		R	A	B	A	T
L		E		M		L		R		D		R		I
G	I	L	B	E	R	T		A	L	A	M	E	D	A
O		U		J		I		R		R		S		N
A	L	T	A	I		C	H	A	R	E	N	T	E

EXPLANATIONS
Across: 1 K(hon)K+A+en, 6 Ta+tar, 10 Tire[rev]+anag of 'era', 11 Double def, 13 Ag(-e)+in+court, 14 O(MD)ur+man, 16 Et+Na(-ples) & pun, 20 D+1+SS, 21 MEP[rev]+broke, 24 Anag, 25 RA+bat, 27 Double def & pun, 28 A+la+Med+a, 29 Hidden word in 'ReAL TAlga', 30 Char+en+te(-a).
Down: 2 Homophone (hate+ye), 3/12 Northern+Irish, 4 A+raw+aka+N, 5 [John] Nash+1K, 6 Pun on capital of the state of Mexico in the nation of Mexico!, 7 Anag, 8 Rash+T, 9 Anag, 15 Dash+t+anag of 'lute', 17 A+l(-1)eut+Ian, 18 A+rare+Med [all rev], 19 Double def & pun [ref Aberdare Mts], 22 Initial letters, 23 B(anag of 'ti[-d]al)C, 24 A(l)g(o)a, 26 Bre(-a)st.

17

E		P		G		H		E		P		T		O
C	L	E	V	E	L	A	N	D		A	R	R	A	S
U		R		O		R		G		R		E		S
A	U	S	T	R	A	L		E	L	M	I	N	Y	A
D		I		G		E		H		E		T	
O	S	A	G	E		M	A	I	D	S	T	O	N	E
R		N				L		A					R	A
E	A	S	T	E	R	I	S	L	A	N	D	E	R	S
A			T		T					R				T
N	I	G	E	R	I	A	N	S		C	H	I	N	G
		A		U		B		W		O		T		E
R	O	S	A	R	I	O		E	M	P	E	R	O	R
U		C		I		R		D		T		E		M
H	A	O	R	A		A	M	E	R	I	C	A	N	A
R		N		N		N		I		N		C		N

EXPLANATIONS
Across: 9 Homophone of 'cleave'+land, 10 A+RR+a+s, 11 Austral(-A1[rev]), 12 Elm+in+y+a, 13 O+sage, 14 Maid's+tone, 16 Anag, 20 Niger+i(an)s, 23 Ching(-Ford), 24 'Ro(sari)o, 25 'per' in heart of anag of 'Rome', 26 Homophone of 'how'+Ra, 27 Anag.
Down: 1 Anag, 2 Per+Sian's, 3 G(E)orge, 4 Double def & pun, 5 Edge+hill, 6 Par+anag of 'names', 7 T(rent)o, 8 Pun on highest peaks of the same name, 15 East(G)er+man, 17 Anag, 18 Ita+bora+1, 19 Anag of 'rite'+re+A(-frica)n, 21 Gas+con, 22 Swede+n, 23 Cop+tic, 24 Reversed initial letters.

18

```
R A M S G A T E · S I · V A S
C L · A Y · S Y · I · · A
O S T E N D E · S A R A C E N
M · A · S · R · E · I · T · A
A R S U K · S A N T A R O S A
N · · R · R · · N · R · · ·
C A P R I C O R N · E I G G
H · E · T · C · I · K · A · U
E R N E · · K I L L A R N E Y
· · I · M · · E · L · · · A
B E N L O M O N D · A S P E N
E · S · R · S · E · H · A · E
L A U T O K A · L H A P A S S
E · L · N · K · T · R · R · E
M I A M I · A M A R I L L O
```

EXPLANATIONS
Across: 1 Rams+gate, 6 S(IV+A)S, 10 O(Sten)de, 11 Pun on popular pub name, 12 Anag of 'a Kurs(-k)', 13 Santa+Rosa, 14 Capri+corn, 17 E(1)gg, 20 Hidden word in 'lowER NEwry', 21 Kill+(B+L)arney, 23 Ben+Lomond, 25 As+pen, 27 Anag of 'walkabout' minus 'W'+'B', 28 Lha(-SA)+pass & pun, 29 Mi+ami(-go), 30 Am(a+rill)o.
Down: 2 Hidden word in 'basALT Assemblages', 3 Anag of 'strains' around 'k', 4 Aye(R)s+rock, 5 'E' in 'Ness'[rev] & pun on 'monstrous waters', 6 (-As)Syrian, 7 Double def & pun, 8 S(An[-n]a)A, 9 Co+Manche, 15 Pen+in+(A[I]US, rev], 16 Nile+delta, 18 Guy+a+anag of 'seen', 19 Kal(aha+r)i, 22 Mo(r)on+I, 23 Hidden word in 'MoB ELEMents', 24 OS+aka, 26 Pa(a+R)l.

19

```
· M A U N A L O A · A N G U S
C · N · O · A · L · S L · I
A N G A R S K · E U S K A D I
D · L · S · E · P · I · M · R
I S E R E · C A P E S C O T T
L · · M · H · O · O · I · R
L U T H E R A N · · A G R A
A · A · N · D · P · D · A · T
C O M O · · S A V A N N A H
· · I · A · M · I · L · · E
P A L E M B A N G · M A C O N
U · N · B · N · N · A · A · I
G R A N A D A · T A T A R I A
E · D · T · U · O · I · I · N
T R U R O · S A N D A K A N
```

EXPLANATIONS
Across: 1 Anag of 'manual'+o+a, 6 Homophone & pun on Ab Ang steak, 10 Anag of 'gas+tank' minus 't'+'r', 11 EU+sk(ad)i, 12 1's+ere, 13 Cape+Scott, 14 Lut(h)e+ran & pun on Joe Strummer of The Clash, 16 Ag(-o-)ra, 20 Co+MO=modus operandi, 21 Savanna+h, 24 Pale+m+bang, 25 Double def & pun, 27 Gr+Adana[rev], 28 Tat+aria, 29 Anag of 'R+tour', 30 Sand+a+k(-H)an.
Down: 2 Double def, 3 Anag & lit, 4 La(K+E)Ch+AD, 5 Ale+pp+o, 6 As+Si+Si, 7 Glam+organ, 8 Initial letters, 9 Pun on French regions and the motor car, 15 Anag, 17 Double def, 18 Homophone of 'pain'+'heavy+weight', 19 Anag, 22 Am(bat)o, 23 Hidden word, in 'woMAN AUStralian', 24 Double def, 26 Car(1)a.

20

```
· E D M O N T O N · P A T N A
B · U · O · U · A · U · O · L
E L B A S A N · G R E N A D A
A · A · T · I · O · B · M · N
U D I N E · S C Y L L A A N D
V · N · I · A · O · S · · N
A R C A D I A N · · N I S H
I · H · E · N · B · P · N · A
S I A M · · C A T A L A N S
· · R · W · A · L · L · · T
Z U Y D E R Z E E · M A S A I
O · B · N · A · A · D · W · N
M A D I S O N · R E A D I N G
B · I · U · I · I · L · S · S
A K S U M · A L C H E V S K
```

EXPLANATIONS
Across: 1 Not(no+MD)e [all rev], 6 Pat+n/a, 10 Elba's+an, 11 Grenad(-e)+a, 12 U+dine, 13/15 Anag, 14 A+r+cad+Ian, 16 Sin[rev]+H, 20 Hidden word in 'TuniSIA Maybe', 21 Cat+Alans, 24 Homophone of Z-ider+Z-ee & pun, 25 Ma(SA)i, 27 Mad+I+son, 28 Double def & pun, 29 A(K)sum, 30 Anag of 'Check+Slav' minus 'c'.
Down: 2 Dub+A1, 3 Pun on Flemish spelling, 4 Tun+is+1+a+n, 5 Na(go)y+a, 6 Double def, 7 Anag, 8 A+land & pun, 9 Beau+VA+is, 17 Ha(sting)s, 18 Anag, 19 Palm+(E+lad [rev]), 22 New[rev]+sum, 23 A+homophone of 'zany'+A, 24 Z(-ambi)(o+MB)a, 26 Homophone of 'roll' & pun on Swiss roll.

21

```
  A B A             I
A R K A N S A S   F R A N C E
  C   N   T   H   R   R   H
  T I G H I N A   E L A Z I G
  I   U       S   M   L   K
C H I H U A H U A     S A A R
      L   I       N   E   W
C O G N A C     O T T A W A
H   U   N   E       L
M E S A   B A R C E L O N A
T   R   A   E       G   N
K U W A I T     B E L F A S T
M   N   O   U   Y   D   R
N A P I E R     S L O V E N I A
L               N   N   M
```

22

```
  C A U C A S I A   C O C O S
F   T   O   C   N   H   H   L
A N T A L Y A   K R A J I N A
L   E   O       P   A   S   V
K O R O R   A F R I K A A N S
L   A   B   A   A   G
A R C A D I A N       D O R T
N   A   O   Y   B   B   A   A
D U R G       S A V A N N A H
    I   Z   G   I   R   I
D J A J A P U R A   C A B O T
A   C   M   Y   M   E   A   I
C O I M B R A   A T L A N T A
C   C   I   N   R   O   D   N
A M A P A   A M E R S H A M
```

23

```
E T H N I C C L E A N S I N G
A   A   O   U   V   E   S   R
S U R I N A M   E L S T R E E
T   V   A   B   R   S   A   A
S A A R   T R I E R   L E T T
I   R   K   I   S   N   L   C
B A D U L L A   T H E L I D O
E       A           P       R
R Y B I N S K   C H A D I A N
I   L   G   O   H   L   P   I
A F A R   C R O A T   L A O S
N   S   B   E   N   F   N   L
S A K A R Y A   G R E V E N A
E   E   A   N   J   N   M   N
A N T I C O S T I   I S L A N D
```

EXPLANATIONS

Across: 5 Anag of 'sank'+'Saar', 7 F+Rance & lit, 9 Tigh(-t)+in+a, 10 Ale[rev]+zig(-zag), 11 Double def & pun, 13 Homophone of 'tsar', 14 Cog+anag of 'can', 16 A+Watt+o [all rev], 18 Double def & pun, 19 Anag, 22 Homophone of 'Queue, wait', 23 B+le[rev]+fast, 25 N+(-r)apier, 26 S(love)+Ain[rev].

Down: 1 Arc+tic(-k), 2 Anag & lit, 3 Reversed hidden word in 'AmrITSAr', 4 1+homophone of 'chick'+a+wa(-g), 6 'hash' in 'is' [rev], 7 Fre(-e)+mantle, 8 Anag of 'LA+area's', 12 Anag, 14 C+he(tum)al, 15 Guaran(-tee)+i, 17 Ere+bus, 20 Ago[rev]+den, 21 A+n+trim, 24 (-near)Ly on(-line) & lit.

EXPLANATIONS

Across: 1 C(Au)C+Asia, 6 Co+Co+s, 10 Ant+a+anag of 'lay', 11 Anag of 'Kilimanjaro' minus anag of 'limo', 12 K+RORO [rev], 13 Anag, 14 Arc+a+Dian(-a), 16 Dort(-mund) & diminutive for 'Dordrecht', 20 Du(R)g, 21 Sava+n+Han [rev], 24 Anag of 'Padua+jar' around 'J', 25 Reversed initial letters, 27 Co+(1+m)bra, 28 Atla(-s)+NT+a, 29 A+map+a, 30 Am(ER+sh)am.

Down: 2 Hidden word in 'mATTERhorn', 3 Double def & pun, 4 S+cap+a+bay, 5 Homophone of 'anchor'+a, 6 Chas[-e]+K[-iow]a, 7 Anag & pun on L Michigan, 8 S(l)A(v)S, 9 Homophone of 'fork'+land, 15 c(aria)c+i+CA, 17 Anag, 18 BA+A1[rev]+mare, 19 Barcelo(-n/a)'s, 22 Z(a+MB)ia', 23 Guy+an+A, 24 D+A/C+rev [ref old spelling of Dhaka], 26 B+and+A.

EXPLANATIONS

Across: 1 Anag, 9 Su(anag of 'rain')m & play on anag indicator, 10 [Ernie] Els+tree, 11 Homophone of 'tsar', 12 Double def & pun of wine tasting, 13 Let+T & lit, 16 BA+dull+a, 17 Anag, 18 Ry+bins+K, 21 C+Had(-R)ian, 23 Double def, 24 C+(-g)roat, 25 Reversed hidden word in 'alSO ALarming', 28 Sa(k)ar+y+a, 29 Anag, 30 Anti+cost+1+island.

Down: 1 Anag, 2 Pun, 3 Io+NA, 4 Cu+MB+air[rev], 5 Eve+rest, 6 NE+SS, 7 (-D)Israeli, 8 Anag, 14 Pun, 15 Anag & pun, 19 B(l)asket, 20 KO+re+a+N-S & pun, 21 Ch+a+n+anag of 'jig', 22 I'(pane)m+a, 26 Brac(-e), 27 Initial letters.

24

E	P	I	S	C	O	P	A	L	I	A	N		
V		K		H		A		I		L		M	T
O	N	E	G	A		L	O	N	G	B	E	A	C	H
R		D		L		K		Z		I		K	A
A	L	A	G	O	A	S				O	G	A	K	I
		S		T		M		N		S			L
G	U	L	F	S	T	R	E	A	M		O	S	S	A
L		A		E		A	T		T		A		N
A	U	C	H		K	I	R	O	V	O	G	R	A	D
C		I		M		T		G		R			
E	R	O	D	E			R	O	S	E	T	T	A
B		T		K		M		O		H		U	U
A	L	A	B	A	M	A	N	S		A	H	L	E	N
Y		T		L		L		S		V		S	I
		C	A	M	E	R	O	O	N	I	A	N	S

EXPLANATIONS

Across: 1 Anag of 'policies Japan' minus 'J', **9** One+G(eorgi)a, **10** Long+Beach, **11** a+la+Goa+S, **12** 1+G+ago [all rev], **14** Pun, **16** Hidden word in 'TrOSSAchs', **18** Au+Ch, **19** Anag, **21** Double def, **22** Rose+Etta, **26** Anag, **27** A(h)le+N, **28** Came+roo(N+Ian)s.
Down: 1 'Or' in Ave'[rev], **2** IKE(d)A, **3** Anag of 'slot-machines' minus anag of 'mint', **4** Pal(k)s'+trait, **5** Double def + pun [ref: Mozart's Symph No 36 (Linz) & his death, aged 35], **6** A+l(B)ion, **7** MA+SS in anag of 'Kara', **13** Anag, **14** G(lace+BA)y, **15** La+C(1)ot+at, **17** Tor(shav[-e])y, **20** Anag of 'Male' around a+K[rev], **23** Pun on the Gene Pitney hit & the R&Ham musical, **24** Aun(-t)+is, **25** Double def & pun on removing the accent.

25

EXPLANATIONS

Across: 1 Anag of 'Balearic'+A, minus 'E', **6** BA+ant[rev], **10** A+rap+a+Ho(-pi), **11** L(is)B+urn, **12** Ala+Mo, **13** El Al+am+E+in, **14** Initial letters, **16** Is+is, **20** Hidden word in 'anorAKS Usually', **21** Lark[rev]+(-Sara)jevo, **24** c+Umbrians, **25** Double definition + pun, **27** Anag & pun on Laramie's wicked past, **28** 'bar' in homophone of 'Iraqi', **29** Assen(-t), **30** [Jennifer] An(n)iston
Down: 2 Hidden word in 'BetrAYAL Accusation' & pun on warm wind, **3** Amazon+as, **4** Rhodes+A1[rev] & lit, **5** all+Gau(-l), **6** Anag, **7** Anag, **8** Initial letters & lit, **9** A+WA+Z(an)aK[all rev], **15** Anag & lit, **17** 'Oven' in 'ails'[rev], **18** P+Russian & pun on historic perceptions, **19** Al(ask)an's, **22** Br+(e)men, **23** Gale+N(-ebrask)a [ref base for 18th C pioneers], **24** Co(L)ca, **26** Anag of 'h'+'coca'.

26

EXPLANATIONS

Across: 5 Homophone of 'See you'+dad & pun on historical name, **8** Den+Ali [Aleutian name for Mt McKinley], **9** Pun on the home of the Marquis of Bath, **10** Sh(1)a(-h), **11** Anag, **12** EP+in+a+l, **14** B(Asti)A, **17** Anag, **20** Hidden word in 'heEL EAgerly', **21** Double def & pun on John Churchill, 1st Duke of Marlborough, **22** Double def , **23** Anag.
Down: 1 'a+hat' in anag of 'wig' around 'U', **2** K(a+rib)(-aund)a, **3** Anag of 'manual'+o+a, **4** Double def & pun, **5** Pun, **6** Gil(-ead)+boa, **7** Anag of 'cream teas at' around 'ad', **13** Angles+ey(-ed) & lit, **15** The+[William] Hague, **16** K+rim+ml, **18** Not+Nag[both rev], **19** A(n)gora.

27

```
P O T O M A C ■ D E R B E N T
■ D ■ R ■ L ■ G ■ T ■ U ■ A ■
C A L I ■ I S L E O F J U R A
■ W ■ Y ■ G ■ O ■ S ■ U ■ M ■
M A L A G A ■ B A H A M I A N
■ R ■ R ■ R ■ A ■ A ■ B ■ D ■
B A D O N H I L L ■ P U S A N
■ ■ ■ C ■ W ■ ■ ■ R ■ ■ ■ ■ ■
K O P E K ■ P A I S V A S C O
■ K ■ A ■ P ■ R ■ I ■ R ■ ■ ■
M A N N H E I M ■ A C A D I A
■ Y ■ S ■ L ■ I ■ M ■ N ■ M ■
P A R I S I E N N E ■ G E E Z
■ M ■ D ■ O ■ G ■ S ■ E ■ A ■
M A Y E N N E ■ B E L L U N O
```

EXPLANATIONS

Across: 1 Po+to+Cam[rev], 5 Derb(-y)+anag of 'ten', 10 Cal+I, 11 Anag, 12 M(a+lag)A, 13 Bah+ami+a+n, 14 BA+don+hill, 16 P+USA+N, 17 KO+Pek(-ing), 19 Anag, 23 Mann+He(l)m, 24 ACA+aid[rev], 26 Paris+1+palindrome of 'NE', 27 Homophone of 'Jeez' & pun, 28 may+E+N+NE, 29 Bell+uno.

Down: 2 o+d+a+war+a, 3 Hidden word in 'AudiO RIYADh', 4 Anag, 6 Et+anag of 'Xhosa' minus 'X', 7 Bu(-m)+J(U+MB)ura, 8 N+armada, 9 Double def & lit, 18 Okay+a+M(-azd)a, 20 Anag, 21 Crime+a+N, 22 PE+lion, 25 Double def.

28

```
B A H R A I C H ■ O J I B W A
A ■ A ■ D ■ H ■ Y ■ U ■ R ■ Z
T S U N A M I ■ O S T R A V A
M ■ S ■ M ■ P ■ R ■ E ■ G ■ N
A R A B S ■ P A K I S T A N I
N ■ S ■ T ■ I ■ S ■ ■ N ■ A ■
■ ■ M O U N T H E L I C O N ■
B ■ I ■ W ■ G ■ I ■ E ■ A ■ S
A N T A N A N A R I V O ■ ■ ■
D ■ A ■ O ■ E ■ I ■ ■ B ■ O ■
L E N I N G R A D ■ T R I E R
A ■ A ■ E ■ T ■ A ■ T ■ H ■ E
N E G O M B O ■ L U O Y A N G
D ■ A ■ E ■ N ■ E ■ W ■ R ■ O
S Y R I A N ■ A S U N C I O N
```

EXPLANATIONS

Across: 1 Anag of 'a Bihar'+Ch, 5 Initial letters, 10 'man'[rev] in anag of 'suit', 11 Hidden word in 'glasnOST RAVAging', 12 A+bar[rev]+S, 13 P(a+kis(-s)+tan)i, 14 Mount+helico(-pter)+N & pun on the mythical home of the Muses, 18 Anag, 21 Lenin+grad(-e), 23 Double def, 24 Anag, 25 L(you[rev])ang, 26 (-As)Syrian, 27 A+s(UN)cion.

Down: 1 Double def & pun, 2 Hau(SA)s, 3 Adam's+town, 4 Chipping+Norton, 6 Jute+S, 7 B+rag+an+CA, 8 (+T)A(-n)zanians, 9 Anag, 15 Levit(-e)+town, 16 Pun on bad+lands, 17 1+tan+anag of 'raga', 19 b(1+h)ar+I, 20 Ore+gon(-e), 22 'E' in 'amen' [rev].

29

```
■ A ■ J ■ B ■ ■ M ■ H ■ L
H Y D E P A R K ■ A B O M E Y
■ M ■ N ■ C ■ E ■ L ■ T ■ M
G A Z A ■ C I R C A S S I A N
■ R ■ ■ A ■ A ■ N ■ P ■ R ■
C A N C E R ■ L I G U R I A N
■ ■ H ■ A ■ A ■ ■ I ■ I ■
■ D U A R T E ■ R E N N E S
■ I ■ F ■ A ■ L ■ G ■
A N N A R B O R ■ F O S H A N
■ D ■ R ■ E ■ M ■ A ■ G ■
K I R I T I M A T I ■ A G A U
■ G ■ N ■ R ■ G ■ Y ■ G ■ D
N U M A Z U ■ H A U T R H I N
■ L ■ S ■ T ■ ■ M ■ I ■ R
```

EXPLANATIONS

Across: 7 H(-ideawa)y+de+park, 9 A+b(OM)ey, 10 Double def & pun, 11 C+1+RC+anag of 'Asians', 12 Double def & pun, 14 Anag, 15 Du(art)e, 16 Homophone of 'wren', 19 Ann+arbor, 21 F(OS+H)an, 23 Kiri[Te Kanawa]+tim L(A GA)u, 24 A(GA)u, 25 N(um+A+Z)u, 26 Anag of 'unhealthier' minus anag of 'Lee'.

Down: 1 A+y+(a+ram[rev]), 2 J(en)a, 3 Double def, 4 M(Alan)G, 5 Homophone of 'geysers' & pun, 6 Anag, 8 Hidden word in 'worKER ALARming', 13 Anag & lit, 15 Din+dig+U+L, 17 Anag, 18 Arm+a+g(-irlis)h, 20 B(Eir[-e])ut, 22 GA[rev](ad)RI[rev], 24 Agri(-culture).

30

```
      B  M        C  L
C  H  O  O  Y  U     M  O  O  S  E  J  A  W
   O     G     T  U     O     N     I     M
A  N  D  A  M  A  N  S     T  A  R  S  U  S
   D     Z     R     A     A     I        R
M  U  C  K  L  E  F  L  U  G  G  A
   R     O           A        A     E     G
K  A  L  Y  A  N           M  O  B  I  L  E
   S        A     H           E     E     E
      G  O  N  D  W  A  N  A  L  A  N  D
G     Y     C     A     E     L           S
D  U  L  U  T  H     N  E  W  D  E  L  H  I
A     M     O     G     H     I           E
A  M  I  R  A  N  T  E     A  L  L  I  E  R
      I     G                 M     E
```

EXPLANATIONS

Across: 5 Choo(-choo)+y(-o)u, **7** Moo(SE) Jaw & pun on the two Londons, **9** (-P)Anda(man)s, **10** Tars+US, **11** Muck+el[rev]+F+anag of 'Gaul' around 'G', **13** Homophone of 'Kali'+an, **15** Double def & pun, **18** Gon(-e)+anag of 'wand'+A+land, **21** Du+Luth(-eran), **22** Anag, **23** Amir+ante, **24** All(1)er.

Down: 1 Bog+a(z(OK[rev])y, **2** Double def & pun on Latin verb 'to change', **3** Con+t+a+gem, **4** [Princess] Le(IR)ia, **6** Anag, **7** Sum[rev]+A(l)A, **8** A+rum[rev], **12** Glen's+hee(-l) [ref to US singer Glen Campbell] **14** Na(n+Ch+on)g, **16** B(elle)ile, **17** Anag of 'Newha(-m)' around 'G', **18** Anag, **20** 'a' in 'mug' [rev].

31

```
   M     G     L        A     B     L
S  A  M  A  R  A     M  A  R  I  A  N  A  S
   L     S     N        U     A     N     T
L  A  O  T  I  A  N  S     G  R  A  H  A  M
   B     O     R        C     U     B     K
M  A  U  N  A  K  E  A     A  L  A  N  I  A
   R     I        T        I        A     A
      P  A  N  A  M  A  C  A  N  A  L
   G        R     N              B     H
C  U  I  A  B  A     D  E  B  R  E  C  E  N
   J     Z     P        O     E     R     M
L  A  D  O  G  A     M  B  A  N  D  A  K  A
   R     R     H        A     U     A     U
C  A  P  E  H  O  R  N     C  O  R  O  N  A
   T     S     S        E     E     D
```

EXPLANATIONS

Across: 7 Samar(-1)a, **8** Maria(n+a)'s, **9** Anag, **10** Gr(a+H)am, **11** Anag & lit, **12** Alan+A1[rev], **13** Anag of 'Alpaca+Ann' around 'am', **18** Cu(1+A)ba, **20** Anag of 'corned beef' minus 'FO', **22** Lad+ago[rev], **23** M+band+aka, **24** Anag, **25** Double def.

Down: 1 Lam[rev]+a+bar, **2** GA's+Tonia, **3** L(a+n)ark, **4** Ar(agua)ia, **5** Ban+a+BA, **6** Anag, **8** Anag, **14** A+rap+Pa(-p)hos, **15** A(be)+Rd+A+re, **16** G(-uangzho)u+jar+at, **17** Hem+K+und, **19** A+z+ores, **21** Beau+CE & pun on the 'breadbasket of France'.

32

```
N  O  U  M  E  A     C  Y  C  L  A  D  E  S
   K     I     V        O     A     T     S
M  A  N  N  H  E  I  M     M  O  H  A  C  S
   R     A     Y        E     S     A     O
M  A  A  S  T  R  I  C  H  T     B  R  N  O
         O        O        E     A     D
I  N  D  I  A  N  A  N        R  U  S  S  I  A
   O     R                    C     D
A  T  T  I  C  A     K  R  A  K  A  T  O  A
   R     A     D        A     R
L  E  O  N     Z  I  M  B  A  B  W  E  A  N
   D     J     H        P     F     R     R
B  A  M  A  G  A     A  M  U  D  A  R  Y  A
   M     Y     R        L     R     T     A
S  E  R  A  M  S  E  A     A  T  H  E  N  S
```

EXPLANATIONS

Across: 1 Anag, **5** Cycl(AD)es, **9** Man+n+h(E)im, **10** Anag & pun on battle in 1526 when Hungary fell to the Ottomans, **11** Maas+T(rich)T, **12** B+RN+o, **13** In+Diana+n, **16** (-P)Russia, **17** Attic+a, **19** Anag of 'OT+ark+aka' & pun, **21** Noel[rev], **22** Anag, **25** B+(Agama[rev]) [ref northernmost settlement in Oz], **26** A+Mu+anag of 'a+yard', **27** Se(R)a(M)+sea, **28** Anag & lit.

Down: 2 Ok(a)ra, **3** Hidden word in 'vitaMIN ASsignments', **4** Av(eyr[-e])on, **5** Come(C)+on, **6** Cam(ST)er(-a), **7** Anag of 'chats' about 'a+BA'+a, **8** E+S+con+Dido, **14** Notre+dame, **15** 1+anag of 'Aryan+I' around 'Ja', **18** Anag, **19** K(amp)ala(-hari), **20** A+RAF+Ura(-l), **23** Double def, **24** Initial letters.

33

EXPLANATIONS

Across: 8 Ja(-p+V)anese, **9** Anag, **10** Cob[rev]+age, **11** N+E+W+S+tea+d, **12** Anag of 'alas'+me+er, **13** To+bag+o, **14** Anag, **18** A(ran)da, **20** A+n(a+dark)o & lit [ref founded as Wichita Indian Agency in 1859], **23** 'a+Nell' in 'ill' [rev], **24** Initial letters & pun on 'first', **25** Ban+ten [ref former name was 'bantam' which gave name to fowl], **26** Ch+alde(-RM)an.

Down: 1 Bar+ado[rev], **2** M+anag of 'arak' around 'a+SS', **3** Anag of 'meek'+le, **4** Double def, **5** Anag, **6** Can+tab, **7** Man[rev]+a+anag of 'gang', **15** Au+rill+a+C, **16** Homophone of 'tsarland', **17** Pun on Snake & Anaconda rivers, **19** N+(-t)enets, **21** Double def , **22** Kangar(-[o-o]).

34

EXPLANATIONS

Across: 1 Anag+E+S & lit [ref to the erratic flow of the R Darling], **10** El+Che + pun, **11** E(-s)leuth+era, **12** Villa+Ch, **13** A(orang[-e])1, **14** Palindrome of 'val', **16** Anag, **19** Can(A+KK)al+E, **20** Ca+LVI+pun (Nelson lost an eye in the siege of 1794), **22** S(-C+1K)hism, **25** Lar(is)s+a, **27** A+mag+a+saki, **28** MBE+y+a, **29** Pun on 'La Manche'.

Down: 2 Anag, **3** NZ+eg+a, **4** Elephant+a, **5** S(1)+E+N+a, **6** Anag of 'cart in 'antic', **7** Double def & pun, **8** SW (-AR)abian, **9** Y+'liv(o)e'[rev], **15** Lake+1+Iran [rev], **17** Been+Leigh [ref to rum distillery here], **18** Double def, **19** Double def, **21** I(bad)an, **23** Hidden word in 'KazaKH ARGentinean, **24** (-H+M)eath [Erica is the botanical name for heath], **26** Roman(-s).

35

EXPLANATIONS

Across: 8 Hidden word in 'ChristMAS A DAnger', **9** Las(vega[-n])s, **10** P(is)A, **11** Anag, **12** (-Cala+Um)bria, **14** Ball+a+rat, **15** Anag of 'Darfur' minus 'D'+'r', **16** E+tang, **18** Far+S, **19** King+ston(-e), **22** Ami+en+S, **23** Micro+NE+Sia(-m), **25** aka+N, **27** Anag of 'Ulan Bator', minus anag of 'ran', around 'way', **28** A+lago(-o)n.

Down: 1 N(A+Z)I, **2** A+lac[rev]+br(1)a, **3** Palm+dale, **4** Initial letters, **5** Reversed hidden word in 'cLEAR SIngle-mindedness', **6** Belay+a, **7** La(Ke[-y]Na)t(-E)r+on, **13** Martini+que, **14** Bear+N, **17** Anag of 'hang+a'+1+A, **18** Zia+F[both rev]+a+bad, **20** German(-E), **21** Tong+a+n, **24** Double def & pun, **26** A/C+Or.

36

EXPLANATIONS

Across: 7 BA+Jan, 8 Anag of 'ban+guava'+y, 10 La+re-do, 11 (-H)Adria(-n)+tic, 12 K(-eny)a+B(a+leg)A, 13 A(ks)U, 15 Borne+an, 17 Maya+pan, 20 Pun, 22 Major+can, 25 C(a+lam)at+a, 26 May+tab[all rev], 27 Anag, 28 Homophone of 'candy'.

Down: 1 Gal(a+p+ago)s, 2 Male+anag of 'Goa'+n, 3 Anna+Jaf(-fa), 4 Anag of 'laird'+a+da(-m), 5 (-k+d)ayaks, 6 Carib(-bean), 9 Bo(-1)se, 14 Bar+a+c+al(-e)+do, 16 Ash+(Ta+bag[both rev]), 18 Anag of 'amir'+tsar, 19 Am+(C[Ira]h, all rev), 21 Pun on resting place after the Flood, 23 Ju(-R+B)a, 24 Navaj(-o).

37

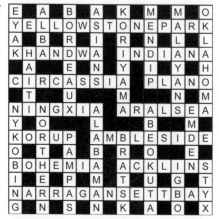

EXPLANATIONS

Across: 9 Yellow+stone+park, 10 Khan+anag of 'wad(-1)', 12 In+Diana, 13 Anag of 'crisis' around 'ca'+A, 14 Plan+O, 15 N+in+G(XI)A, 18 Anag of 'as real (-as) a', 21 Homophone of 'corrup(-t)', 23 Ambles+I'd+e, 25 Pun, 26 Ac(k+nil[rev])s, 29 Anag of 'aberrant+nasty' around 'Ag'.

Down: 1 E+yak, 2 A+lb+A, 3 B(o+Rd)eaux, 4 A+Sian's, 5 Anag, 6 Men(-d)+dip, 7 Malay(an)s, 8 Double def, 11 Ha(l)t+l, 15 NY+KO+Bing, 16 Anag, 17 A+l+a+BA+man, 19 Abe+OK+Uta(-h), 20 Me+den, 22 Pam(Pa)'s, 24 Brats+K, 27 Hidden word in 'bIG BOys', 28 Homophone of 'sticks'.

38

EXPLANATIONS

Across: 6 Cut+tack, 7 Homophone of 'pool', 9 Homophone of 'pukey'!, 10 Anag, 11 Mal(a+t)aya, 13 Tu(are)g, 15 Al(-a)bi, 17 Pun on occupations in the Six Days and Yom Kippur Wars, 18 Got+h, 19 Go+M+era, 20 Anag, 23 Pun, 26 O(A)il[rev], 27 Hidden word in 'XanADU WAy', 28 Ge(-t)+henna.

Down: 1 Anag, 2 Fa(-n)+E+NZ+a, 3 A(-las[-s])kan, 4 Apple+anag of 'ton', 5 (-Laio)dong, 6 Cauca(-[S+US]), 8 Ever+E+TT, 12 Anag, 14 A+n+g(U)ill+ans, 16 R+y in anag of 'a+loo'+A, 17 Gram+p(1)an & pun following last clue, 21 (i)l(e)S(h)a, 22 A(Mas[rev])a, 24 Homophone of 'nook', 25 Lug+o.

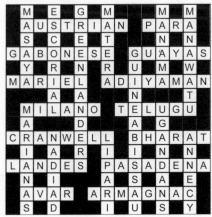

39

EXPLANATIONS

Across: 1 Double def, 5 Les+bo(-y)s, 10 l(O)i(r)e, 11 Anag & pun on Lennon's 'Norwegian Wood' & Ron Wood of Faces & R Stones fame, 12 A+com+A+rock, 13 Han+o+i, 14 Law+to+n, 15 N+a+NY+(-anag) & pun on 'Chinatown', 18 Easter+N, 20 Bra(oz[rev])s, 22 l(Ah)+do, 24 Homophone & double pun on 'bark'+shire, 25 Ale+U+anag of 'saint', 26 Ami+sh, 27 I+Barra, 28 Anag.

Down: 1 Hidden word in 'IstanBUL GARden', 2 Anag, 3 Fremantle+doctor, 4 Ran+goon, 6 Elephant+A+is+land, 7 Be(1)an, 8 SA+NT+Iago, 9 Anag, 16 Ab(origin)e, 17 Mexic(-o)+Ali, 19 Nub+I+an, 20 Ba(Ross)a, 21 Les+ Han, 23 Aden+a.

40

EXPLANATIONS

Across: 1 Anag, 6 BA+Lt, 9 Lands+krona, 10 y+ale, 12 Kr+anag of 'jog+Ankaras', 15 Pun on ancients' entrance to the underworld & Naples' Mafia connection, 16 A+t+t+(-C)airo, 17 G([-f]ires)un, 19 Colon+A1[rev], 20 Anag & pun of the Passion Plays held there every 10 years since 1634, 23 Anag, 24 Jui(-n)+z+DE(for)A, 25 er(N)e, 26 Homophone of 'Finns' & 'Lap+land+ERs' & pun on King Cnut's lesson.

Down: 1 Double def, 2 A+R+anag of 'on', 3 Anag & lit, 4 A(k)ran+E+S, 5 Tun(is+1)a, 7 Amaz(-ie[rev])onians, 8 Pun on 'The' & Civil War, 11 Cast+ill+ale+O+N, 13 Anag, 14 Georg+Eto(w)n, 18 al(U)p+man [all rev], 19 Cor(Oz)al, 21 Double def, 22 MA+a+s.

41

EXPLANATIONS

Across: 7 Austr(-al)ian, 8 Para(-graph), 9 Anag, 10 Gu(a)y+a+S, 11 Mar+ie+l, 12 A+DIY(A)+man, 13 Hidden word in 'TaMIL ANOther', 14 Anag, 16 C+ran+well, 19 B(-1)har+a+t, 21 Land+E+S, 22 PA+SA+den+a, 23 A+Var, 24 Anag of 'Magna Car(-ta)'.

Down: 1 Nearly a homophone of 'Messiah', 2 Esc+or(1)al, 3 Green+landers & pun, 4 Mat+era, 5 (-p+M)anama, 6 Man+a+W+at+U, 10 Guinea+B+is+s+Au, 13 Mari(A)nas, 15 Anag, 17 Hidden word in 'PooNA DIADem', 18 Initial letters, 20 (-N)An(N+E)cy.

42

EXPLANATIONS

Across: **7** Hidden word in 'DA(-n)+KARate', **8** Double def, **10** Anag, **11** A(RU[rev])1+(-Co)gnac, **12** Cat(Alan)s, **13** U+set[rev], **15** Ram[rev]+a+MBA, **17** A(n+du)jar, **20** If+NI & pun, **22** Ira(oil+K[both rev])n, **25** Double def, **26** Hidden word in 'severAL PINEwoods', **27** Con+naught & pun on spell, **28** D(o)u(r)o.

Down: **1** Malaya+lam(-b), **2** Anag of 'gamay'+a+t+a, **3** B+Ry(a+n)s+k, **4** Anag of 'An+Air+UK' around 'O', **5** I+bag+anag of 'EU', **6** Initial letters, **9** Ba(L)a, **14** Anag, **16** Double def & pun on the launching site for cosmonauts of the past, **18** All+U[both rev]+pool, **19** Hit+a+chi, **21** F(re+S+N)O, **23** B(a)SA[rev], **24** Par+OS.

43

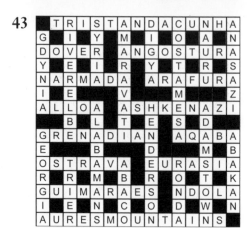

EXPLANATIONS

Across: **1** Anag, **10** d+over, **11** Anag, **12** N+armada, **13** A+RAF+Ura(-I), **14** Pun on close homophone, **16** Double def [ref Vladimir Ashkenazi], **19** Grenad(-[1+ER])+lan, **20** a+Q+a+BA, **22** Anag of 'rotas'+VA, **25** Anag of 'sea+air' around 'U', **27** Gu(I'm+a+RA)es(-s), **28** n(dol[-lar])a, **29** A+anag of 'rest+ unanimous'.

Down: **2** Anag of 'relieve+BR', **3** Hidden word in 'mesSY RIAls', **4** A+mar+avat(-Ra[rev])+1, **5** Did+Y(-orub)a, **6** Cost+a+mesa, **7** Reversed initial letters & lit, **8** A+Na(S+A)zi, **9** Anag of 'Digya+n', **15** Double def & pun on 'red', **17** Anag of 'herons+end', **18** Adam's+town & lit pun on [Fletcher] Christian, **19** a(i)g(r)o(e)G [all rev], **21** Homophone of 'Abba can', **23** Double definition, **24** AB+a+Co, **26** Reversed hidden word in 'rADNORshire'.

44

EXPLANATIONS

Across: **1** KO+Rd+O+fan, **5** Alt+CIA[rev], **9** Ham+[David] Mamet, **10** UN+GA+VA, **12** Mo(NZ)a, **13** Anag & pun on 'exploited', **14** Ba(ja)ns, **16** Let+ICI+a, **19** Las+C+aux, **21** H(-ysteri)a+rare, **23** 'am' in anag of 'landing', **25** Hidden word in 'fOR A PArt', **26** Anag, **27** Mil(a+N)es+e, **28** Old+ham, **29** Double def & pun on former bike racing there.

Down: **1** K(-eral)(o+him)a, **2** (-G)r(Omani)a(-z)+N+S, **3** (-T)Omaha(-wk), **4** (-t)avern+US, **6** Double def, **7** A+MA+SA [all rev], **8** C+anag of 'Handel' around 'a', **11** Initial letters, **15** Anag of 'AA+whisk+A+a', **17** Cart(Agen)a, **18** Ale+N+Tejo, **20** XI+a+n, **21** Anag of 'Dido+he'+a, **22** Ka(-li)+anag of 'rive(-r)', **24** A+land & lit, **25** O+hat+a.

45

```
V I A E M I L I A ■ O L M E C
A ■ R ■ O ■ A ■ O ■ I ■ B ■ O
R O M A N ■ C H R I S T I A N
N ■ E ■ T ■ H ■ A ■ E ■ N ■ C
A R N H E M L A N D ■ ■ V I G O
■ I ■ G ■ A ■ G ■ N ■ ■ ■ ■ R
I D A H O A N ■ I R E L A N D
C ■ N ■ B ■ ■ ■ W ■ N ■ ■ ■ I
E U S K A R A ■ M A G A D H A
L ■ ■ Y ■ T ■ O ■ R ■ A ■ ■ ■
A B C D ■ G L E N E A G L E S
N ■ O ■ C ■ A ■ T ■ N ■ U ■ I
D A R B H A N G A ■ A I S E N
I ■ A ■ I ■ T ■ N ■ D ■ I ■ A
C O L O N ■ A D A P A Z A R I
```

EXPLANATIONS

Across: **1** Anag o 'a+vile+aim' around '1', **6** Ol(-d)+me(-n)+C, **9** Double def & pun on Roman alphabet, **10** Double def, **11** Arnhem, land! & pun on Operation MG, 'a bridge too far', **12** Vigo(-ang of 'sour'), **14** Ida+Ho+a+n, **15** Ire+land, **17** EU's+Kara [Sea], **19** Anag, **20** ABC+d [ref Ss Andre, Bernardo & Caetano with Diadema, cities which surround São Paulo], **22** Glen(eagle)s, **25** Brad[rev]+hang+a, **26** Hidden word in 'rAISE New', **27** Double def & pun, **28** Ad+anag of 'La Paz+air' minus 'L'.

Down: **1** V(a+RN)A, **2** A+RM+anag of 'insane' & pun on landlocked people, **3** Mont(ego)+bay, **4** La+Ch+lan(-d), **5** Anag of 'Angora'+l, **6** Hidden word in 'frambOISEs' & pun, **7** M(B)ini, **8** Pun on Spanish word and right bank of R Uruguay being in Argentina, **13** New+Granada & pun, **14** Anag, **16** (-s)Andal+US(1)A, **18** Atlant(1+C)+a, **19** Mo(-U)nta(-I)n+a, **21** C+oral & pun, **23** Sin+a+i, **24** Chin(-a).

46

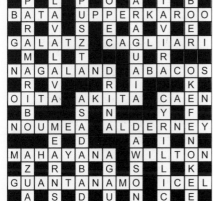

EXPLANATIONS

Across: **8** A+tab[all rev], **9** Anag, **10** Gala+(-gli)tz, **11** Cag(-e)+liar+1, **12** Nag(A)+land & pun on location of clue and def, **14** A+ba(Co)s(-e), **16** Initial letters, **17** ak(it)a, **18** Ca(E)n, **19** No+Umea, **21** Alder+Ney, **23** Ma(h+a)yan+a, **26** Double def & lit, **27** Anag, **28** Icel(-and).

Down: **1** Para+mar+Ibo, **2** Lava-lava & pun, **3** Anag of 'apt' around 'US+z', **4** Pun, **5** Ar(agua)ia, **6** Ta(a+vir)a, **7** re+Ob [all rev]+A, **13** Drin(-k)+A, **15** OK(E+fen)OK+E+E, **17** Homonym of 'Assad'+a+bad, **18** Cyril+l+I/C, **20** M+earns, **22** D(-r)aws+on & pun, **24** A(Zu[-lu])A, **25** Ag+Au.

47

EXPLANATIONS

Across: **1** Anag of 'Jimi+He(=ndrix)', **4** M(a+rat+H)As, **10** Nin(-e)+G+XI+a, **11** G(a+B+Rov[-ER])o, **12** U+Tah([-o+E]), **13** Anag of 'humanitarians' minus 'NHS', **15** Double def & pun, **16** Jam+ai(-d)+CA, **20** A+n+du+Raj [rev], **21** P(a+[art rev])i, **24** Anag, **26** Ham+a & pun on pig iron & steel, **28** Anag of 'Niort' around 'eg', **29** Bur(-y)+K+in+a, **30** A+grin+lo+n, **31** Can+Ada.

Down: **1** Hon+[Roberto]Duran & lit [he was from Panama], **2** Anag of 'boatman' around 'U'+N, **3** J+IX+1, **5** Anger+man, **6** Abbot+taba(-r)d, **7** Ho+or+N & pun, **8** Homonym of Slow+vac, **9** Pat(-h)an, **14** Arauca(-r+n)ia+N, **17** C+anag of Arica+CIA, **18** Tar(a+p)ot+O, **19** Hi+Malay+A, **22** (-L)Ugan(-O)+da, **23** Jam+B1, **25** Anag of 'Negri(-to)' & pun, **27** Art+A.

48

EXPLANATIONS

Across: 1 Anag, **6** A(pi)A, **9** Au+rang+a+bad, **10** Double def, **12** Anag [ref 'Royal' Lytham & St Annes GC, home to golf's Open Championship 5 times], **14** Anag of 'east' around '1+no[rev]', **15** Can+Cu+n, **16** M(A)u+M(A)u, **17** Hidden rev word in 'panAMA(-H+C)AT Allowing', **19** Anag, **21** O+ban, **22** Anag, **24** Double def, **25** Bulg(-e)+homophone of 'Aryans'.

Down: 1 'a' in 'mug' [rev], **2** A+hr, **3** Winston's+ale+m, **4** Double def & pun on 'Seat', **5** A+W(a+SS)A, **7** Abyss+ In(-d)ian, **11** Anag, **8** Anag, **12** Lit+Hu(A[NI]A)ns, **13** German+town & pun on Irish region of the same name, **17** (A)r(l)B(e)r(+g), **18** Double def & pun on the kikuyu golf course grass in Africa, **20** 1+sis, **23** (-1)ota.

49

EXPLANATIONS

Across: 7 Be+lair, **8** Anagram, **9** Anag of 'mill' around 'a+SS+O', **10** Al(PH)e+n, **11** Chic+layo(-u[-pbea]t), **12** A+N+shun, **13** Homophone of 'Verruca bad?', **18** A+kale+M [all rev], **20** Angle+yes[rev], **22** Double def & pun, **23** [Ted] B(urg[-e])undy, **24** Le(Canne[-s])t, **25** N+ap(-p[ip])les.

Down: 1 Anag of 'housing project' minus anag of 'top guns', **2** Pun, **3** Hidden word in 'dORIS SAcrifice', **4** W+aka+may[rev]+a, **5** Camp+so[rev], **6** Cite+aux, **8** Anag, **14** R(wand)an+S, **15** Are(quip)a, **16** Homophone of 'Devises', **17** Double def & pun, **19** A+bad+an, **21** G(E+Ron)A.

50

EXPLANATIONS

Across: 5 Anag of 'alcoholic' minus' anag of 'Col' [Ref: 'Gang' is alternative name for 'Acholi'], **7** OK+a+van+go, **9** Initial letters, **10** Ride[rev]+NE, **11** Plymouth+rock & pun, **13** Gen+ova, **15** Ne(C[-zech and Denmar]k)ar, **18** Bar+ran+quill+a, **21** Bal(t)i+c, **22** Anag, **23** XI+ang(-ers)+fan, **24** Reversed hidden word in 'secRET EXEcutive'.

Down: 1 Co(qui)mbo, **2** VI+sh+Nu, **3** C(a+pet)ow+N, **4** H+a+wick, **6** Cor(Al+S)e+a, **7** O+lathe & pun on Kansas (-C)city, **8** Go(=a)n+d, **12** Carl+Isle, **14** RA[rev]+anag of 'reef' around 'CI', **16** 'O' in homophone of 'chickpea', **17** Fab[rev]+Fin, **18** Botany (-Bay), **19** Que+Bec, **20** 1+lab (rev).